Sir Basil Liddell Hart and Tanks

Bruce Oliver Newsome, Ph.D.

Sir Basil Liddell Hart and Tanks

by Bruce Oliver Newsome, Ph.D.
www.BruceNewsome.com

Sign up for bonus chapters, photographs, and videos.

Published by: Perseublishing,
PO Box 181802, Coronado, California 92178, United States of America

Copyright © 2024 Bruce Oliver Newsome, Ph.D

All rights reserved. No part of this publication may be reproduced or stored in a retrieval system or transmitted, in any form or by any means, electronic, mechanical, photocopying, recording or otherwise, without prior permission in writing from Tank Archives Press.

HIS027090	HISTORY / Military / World War I	
HIS027100	HISTORY / Military / World War II	
HIS027240	HISTORY / Military / Vehicles	
NHWR5	First World War	
NHWR7	Second World War	
NHWL	Modern warfare	
JWMV	Military vehicles	

ISBN: 978-1-951171-22-3

Front cover: Basil Liddell Hart, at home, circa 1967, from a print that he signed for guests; and the5th Battalion RTC on Penham Down, Salisbury Plain, in 1927.

Acknowledgements

The author wishes to thank:
- Emma De Angelis, Editor, "The Journal of the Royal United Services Institution," for permission to quote from the "Journal"
- Faber & Faber, for permission to quote from "The Real War, 1914-1918" by Basil Liddell Hart
- David Fletcher, Historian, The Tank Museum
- Andrew Hart, patron
- Gemma Hollman, Senior Archives Assistant, Libraries & Collections, Kings College London, for permission to quote from Liddell Hart's papers
- Jonathan Holt, Archives Assistant, The Tank Museum
- Christian Lea, Manchester University Press, for permission to quote from "Men, Ideas and Tanks: British Military Thought and Armoured Forces, 1903-1939" by J. Paul Harris
- Bryn Loyd, Archives Assistant, The Tank Museum
- Scott Meyer, patron
- Sheldon Rogers, Archives Assistant, The Tank Museum
- Katie Thompson, Archives Assistant, The Tank Museum
- Marjolijn Verbrugge, Archive and Supporting Collections Manager, The Tank Museum, for permission to quote from the archives
- David Willey, Curator, The Tank Museum

All photographs are courtesy of The Tank Museum and Bruce Oliver Newsome, Ph.D.

CONTENTS

Acknowledgements	2
Contents	3
Abbreviations	4
Introduction	5
Chapter 1: Pedestrians Before Tanks	7
Chapter 2: JFC Fuller and Liddell Hart	9
Chapter 3: Tank Technologies	14
Tracked Transport	14
Great War Tanks	15
Automotive Technologies	16
Signals and Communications	18
Chapter 4: Heavy Tanks	19
Chapter 5: Tankettes and Carriers	23
Chapter 6: Light Tanks	39
Chapter 7: Medium Tanks	45
Chapter 8: Infantry Tanks	50
Chapter 9: Cruiser Tanks	53
Chapter 10: Motorcycles	59
Chapter 11: Future Tanks	61
Chapter 12: Official Historian of the Tank Arm	63
References	70

ABBREVIATIONS

AFV	armored fighting vehicle
AP	armor-piercing
BEF	British Expeditionary Force
CIGS	Chief of the Imperial General Staff
DDM	Design Department Mechanization, Superintendent of Design
DGFV	Director-General Fighting Vehicles
DME	Director of Mechanical Engineering
DMO&I	Director of Military Operations and Intelligence
DRAC	Director Royal Armoured Corps
DSD	Director of Staff Duties
GHQ	General Headquarters (usually field army or regional echelon)
GSO	General Staff Office
HE	high-explosive
hp	horse-power
HQ	headquarters
in.	inch
IRTC	Inspector Royal Tank Corps
IWM	Imperial War Museum, London
km	kilometers
kmh or kph	kilometers per hour
LH	Liddell Hart
LHCMA	Liddell Hart Centre for Military Archives
MCS	Military College of Science
MEC	(British Army) Middle East Command
mm	millimetres
MP	Member of Parliament
mph	miles per hour
MSS	manuscripts
Panzer	*Panzerkampfwagen* (armored fighting vehicle)
pdr	pounder (a gun; numerical prefix is nominal weight of projectile)
RAC	Royal Armoured Corps
RACTM	Royal Armoured Corps Tank Museum, Bovington, Dorset
RAOC	Royal Army Ordnance Corps
RASC	Royal Army Service Corps
RE	Royal Engineers
RHA	rolled homogenous armour; Royal Horse Artillery
RNAS	Royal Naval Air Service
RTC	Royal Tank Corps
RTR	Royal Tank Regiment
UK	United Kingdom
US(A)	United States (of America)
WD	War Department
WO	War Office
yds.	yards

INTRODUCTION

Sir Basil Liddell Hart (1895-1970) is the strongest influence on Anglophone military thought. From the 1920s, he influenced doctrine, force structure, and acquisitions. By the 1950s, he was the official historian of Britain's tank arm, and the self-declared inventor of Blitzkrieg. He died in 1970, a knight of the realm, feted as the greatest expert on tanks in the world (Newsome 2024a).

Liddell Hart's thinking about tanks is more interesting and varied than he or his disciples portrayed. During the Great War, he advocated for pedestrian infantry as the decisive arm. In the 1920s, he embraced JFC Fuller's call for fully-mechanized combined arms. He even advocated for a small, all-tracked army, on the promise that it could end wars in days. Yet he soon embraced one-man tankettes and fancied that all arms could be amalgamated around them. He campaigned for a ban on tanks weighing more than 5 tons. During the 1930s, he prioritized fast, light tanks, each accommodating only one machine-gun and two men. He promised that they could race around the enemy's front, infiltrate the enemy's rear, raid industry and infrastructure, and return days later, without a battle.

During the Second World War, he realized some of his mistakes, but still complained about heavier tanks, bigger guns, and thicker armor, and reimagined a light tank force for hit-and-run raids.

The first three chapters of this book review Liddell Hart's early preference for pedestrians over tanks, his switch to tanks over pedestrians after contacting JFC Fuller (then the tank arm's most senior officer), and his confused and selective engagement with tank technologies.

Chapters 4 to 10 explain his interwar views on, respectively, current heavy tanks, tankettes and carriers, light tanks, medium tanks, infantry tanks, cruiser tanks, and finally (of all things) motorcycles.

Chapter 11 reviews his post-war thoughts on the future of tanks, and reveals previously overlooked restatements of his interwar views.

Chapter 12 reveals his slow, contentious rebound as official historian of the tank arm. Publicly, he leveraged the work to cement his reinvention as the neglected prophet of the sorts of technologies and doctrines normalized during the Second World War. Privately, as I reveal here for the first time, he was inattentive to the work, and played the principals against each other, except where convenient to his reinvention. Thus, his lessons are hit and miss.

Liddell Hart always prioritized speed and stealthiness, which still deserve our attention. Yet we also need to beware of reductionism to speed and stealthiness, at the expense of other aspects of mobility, survivability, and lethality. Liddell Hart offers insights into the speed of Blitzkrieg, and the stealthiness of raids. However, his opus continues to encourage Western regression to fast charging, light footprint, portability, ready deployability, cost savings, and raiding. These ideals are worthy, but need to be balanced. Against inferior adversaries, in easy terrain, they can be spectacular. Against peer competitors or in difficult conditions, they become costly and indecisive. This book helps us to implement his ideals realistically.

The British Army first sent tanks into action on 15 September 1916 at Flers-Courcelette. Two companies were available, with 53 Heavy Mark I Tanks, of which 4 were declared unfit during preparation, leaving 49 to reach the assembly area, of which 32 reached the starting line. British newspapers first published photographs of tanks on 22 November 1916 (right). Liddell Hart was then convalescing in England, so likely saw these newspapers on the day. He certainly would have heard more about them once he returned to duty (as a trainer) in January 1917. Yet his archives contain no notes on tanks until after the Great War.

Tank crews were expected to dismount their machine-guns to fight on foot, once they had broken down, run out of fuel, or become stuck. In this sense, their vehicles were hybrid tanks/carriers. In November, Captain Gifford Le Q. Martel, a staff officer at Tank Corps HQ, circulated a doctrinal vision of several classes of tank, including supply tanks. Major JFC Fuller joined a month later, effectively as chief of staff. Fuller advocated supply tanks ("tank tenders," in his "Training Note No. 16," of February 1917). In June, he suggested that larger carriers (each seven crewmen) could deposit 20 machine-gunners and five machine-guns between the enemy's frontlines and the enemy's reserves. Tank Corps HQ established an organization for converting Mark I Tanks to carriers. (Each vehicle's armament was reduced to one Lewis machine-gun. "Supply sponsons" of soft steel raised the load rating to 5 long tons.) They were first used in combat on 7 June 1917. From September, a dedicated carrier (Mark IX) was developed from the Mark V. The Mark IX (below) is unique in the series for flat sides (without sponsons), two oval doors in each side, and a flatter nose. The engine was moved forward, the gearbox rearward, and the outer track frames were deleted, to increase internal volume. Girders were added transversely to stiffen the sides and floor. The vehicle was rated for a load of 10 tons or 50 soldiers. Mountings for machine-guns were designed at front and rear (Fuller 1920: 109, 166; 1936: 81, 130; Martel 1931: 53).

CHAPTER 1

Pedestrians Before Tanks

Basil Liddell Hart started his military life as an infantryman, by his own choice. As a trainer, educator, and doctrinist, he championed pedestrian infantry, even going so far as to promise that lighter-equipped pedestrians could restore infantry as the primary arm, without tanks. Later, he misrepresented his early writings as prescriptions for tanks. Almost every follower has peddled his misrepresentation, without reading the originals.

Liddell Hart volunteered for the infantry days after the Great War broke out in August 1914. He first deployed to France a year later. His operational experience was infrequent and short. Each of four rotations into the frontlines ended within days, with his evacuation. Despite contradictory explanations, his injuries were largely psychological. He was evacuated from France for the last time in July 1916 (Newsome 2024a: chapter 4). Nevertheless, one of his third-person biographies suggests that "he participated in the fierce fighting of the battle of the Somme, where the British used tanks for the first time at Cambrai" (1956: 2). In fact, tanks were first used at Flers-Courcelette, 25 miles (40 km) short of Cambrai, on 15 September – two months after he had been evacuated. They were first used at Cambrai on 20 November 1917 – 16 months after he had been evacuated. He recorded nothing about these battles at the time. By 1917, he was busy training pedestrian infantry.

At the end of the war, he joined London Division Headquarters (HQ) to administer education. He spent most of his time at home convalescing and turning his pamphlets on pedestrian training drills (1918a; 1918b; 1918c) into wider doctrine.

His first article helpfully allows for infantry to be supported by "other arms," but does not specify tanks. Rather, he specifies "artillery, mortars, machine-guns, [and] low-flying battle aeroplanes" (1919a: 290).

The second article describes the first article as "sufficient...to enable [a platoon] to tackle with success the normal centre of resistance." It requires a "tank" to carry the platoon's equipment and supplies, but means a carrier variant, which the British Expeditionary Force (BEF) had deployed since 1917. The carriers evolved from Heavy Tanks, and were designated as tanks; the "Mark" number was the only difference in designation. Each extant carrier carried a platoon, and mounted at least one machine-gun, for self-defence. Liddell Hart did not want a vehicle to carry the platoon's men or to mount machine-guns. He imagines the vehicle shielding the men during approaches to the battlefield – but not fighting. The War Department had issued a manual on "Infantry and Tank Cooperation and Training" in March 1918, but he does not require proper tanks to support the infantry, and is explicitly sceptical of "ironclad landships" (1919b: 666-668).

He allows proper tanks to screen the attack and to exploit the breakthrough. The current British medium tanks and French light tanks perform this role, although his articles of these years do not admit any classes. Thus, his writing continues to conflate "tanks" with carriers.

> The infantry combat unit should be armed with them [tanks or carriers] in the same way as they are armed with Lewis [light machine-]guns. This would in no way destroy the utility of the Tank Corps as a separate body, whose energies might be devoted to the development of the sphere of action which would appear to lie before them as advanced guards, in the wider sense, and in following up and reaping the full fruits of a victory. The suggestion is that the infantry combat unit might have one of its sections formed as a tank section and trained in its handling (1919b: 667).

He concludes, "first…that the tank is certain to play an increasingly important part in future war." This is ambiguous, because we cannot be sure whether he means all classes of tank or just carriers. He seems to mean just the carriers, given his second conclusion, "that the infantry must, in some way, be provided with greater striking power if they are to retain their decisive role and not to degenerate into the position of mere moppers-up for the other arms" (1919b: 669).

Fifteen years later, he would claim that this second article "seems to have a chance of fulfillment" if "mobile pill-boxes" (two-man tankettes or machine-gun carriers) would replace all the light machine-guns and a third of the men in each infantry battalion (1935: 194). His memoirs misdescribe the article (1919b) as a proposal for "the combination of a more mobile light infantry with tanks in an integrated tank-and-infantry 'combat unit'," and "that tanks and infantry should be combined in it," akin to British "brigade-sized battle-groups" and US "regimental combat teams" of the Second World War. Further, he claims, it was his "first entry into the field of armoured warfare" (1965: I, 86, 35). Similarly, Brian Bond (1977: 27), a mentee and biographer, misdescribed it as "an article on infantry and tanks in a combined unit." In fact, it does not treat tanks as necessary; it uses "tanks" to mean carriers; and it combines infantry and carriers within platoons, not regiments or brigades. Azar Gat (2000: 1) admitted that Liddell Hart's claim is "misleading."

Liddell Hart's following articles, published in 1920, re-assert pedestrians. They do not assert any necessary role for vehicles. One article lists "tanks" among the "masses of auxiliary fire power" for pedestrian infantry attacks (1920a: 39). "New and improved weapons" (unspecified) are useful to surprise, he writes. However, "dispersion" is his sufficient solution to the "new and improved weapons" (1920a: 32). He welcomes "recent developments in tactics and weapons…in particular the machine-gun and automatic rifle," but again does not mention tanks (1920b: 476). His third article of 1920 lists "tanks" among the infantry's "auxiliary fire power," but perhaps again means carriers (1920c: 694). His fourth article paraphrases the third closely, but deletes the statement about "auxiliary fire power," and leaves "dispersion" as sufficient solution to "modern mechanical weapons of destruction" (1921a: 7). He allows for "fast-moving tanks or other mobile troops" to take over the pursuit of a routed enemy from the infantry battalion (1920a: 42; 1921a: 12; 1921b: 181-182). Yet his memoirs and Brian Bond's biography spin these articles as focused on maneuver by tanks during the attack (1965: I, 31-39; Bond 1977: 24-25). They are not.

By the mid-1920s, Liddell Hart, to his credit, proved receptive to an alternative proposed by JFC Fuller – an all-mechanized combined-arms alternative, centered on tanks, as explained in the next chapter.

CHAPTER 2

JFC Fuller and Liddell Hart

In May 1920, Liddell Hart sent his latest article on pedestrian infantry to JFC Fuller, already famous as the chief staff officer of the wartime Tank Corps. Liddell Hart was seventeen years junior in age, several steps junior in rank, several articles short of Fuller's total, and, by his own admission at the time, intellectually inferior.

> I am writing for the immediate present, while infantry are still considered the chief arm. I feel quite certain that the tank will very soon become the sole arm of importance, if only the authorities will listen to the people with organized brains, which naturally include foresight, of whom you are the chief (to Fuller, 15 June 1920, LHCMA LH 1/302).

In the same month, the first part of Liddell Hart's "man in the dark" doctrine was published by the *National Review* magazine. In July, Liddell Hart mailed the second part. Fuller chastised him for over-optimistic expectations for pedestrian maneuver without close support from other arms, particularly tanks. Over many months, Liddell Hart tried to persuade Fuller that his pedestrian doctrine still counted, but Fuller pointed out that he "underestimated the enormous difficulty of supplying attacking infantry who have effected a penetration" (to LH, 25 August 1920, LHCMA LH 1/302). This went on sporadically for more than 18 months. During a final argument about one of Liddell Hart's drafts for a new article, Liddell Hart swung back and forth, before he conceded:

> Of course although tanks are unquestionably the weapon of the immediate future, man as an individual fighter may be resurrected. The infantryman's justification rests on two factors. He is the smallest target and the most universally mobile of all weapon carriers…The nation which is quickest to realize that the period on which we are entering is the tank era will win the next war…
>
> I am an ardent believer in tanks and only want to be converted entirely. Full conviction is however necessary if one is to be a good advocate… Your arguments are so convincing on the tank v[ersus] other arms as they exist, that I am fain to become a disciple (to Fuller, 16 and 31 January 1922, LHCMA LH 1/302).

In the latter letter, Liddell Hart seeks help to join the Tank Corps. Yet he waited more than a year before making any application, once the arm's permanency was confirmed (as the Royal Tank Corps). His memoirs do not credit Fuller. Here, he claims to have been accepted by the Corps in August 1923, only to fail a medical test in the same month. In fact, his records show that a medical board confirmed annual assessments since 1916 that he was fit for sedentary duties only, due to heart palpitations, for which he himself was the only source. He did not dispute these assessments. In October 1923, the War Office canceled his bid (LHCMA LH 8/301-306; 1965: I, 63).

One unadmitted motive for his conversion to tanks is his disillusionment with the Army's reception to his doctrine. Concurrent with his final embrace of tanks, he submitted a long complaint about military conservatism and professionalism.

> Let us not forget that the decisive new weapon of the Great War, the tank, owed its introduction principally to "amateurs" in the face of stubborn opposition from the supreme professional opinion (1923a: 322).

Indeed, Fuller's and Liddell Hart's stance against military conservatism drew them together, particularly as their military careers stalled, although they cycled back to acrimony as their views of mechanization diverged.

In 1923, Liddell Hart told Fuller that Fuller's lectures to the Staff College "are the most brilliant contribution to scientific military thought that has ever been made." Liddell Hart told a favorite correspondent that Fuller is "the greatest intellectual power I have ever come across, a triton among minnows." In 1925, he saw his first full book into publication, a plagiarism of Fuller's vision of a decisive, all-tracked army. Privately, he placed Fuller top of a list of current officers (to Fuller, 11 April 1923, LHCMA LH 1/302; to J.M. Scammell, 1923, LH 1/622; "My rating of officers," 1925, LH 7/1925/2).

However, within a year, Liddell Hart, now a full-time journalist, became more competitive. In 1926, he commissioned Fuller's wartime deputy, Giffard le Quesne Martel, to write the entry on "Tanks" for *Encyclopaedia Britannica*. In 1927, he commissioned Fuller to write the entry on "Cavalry," in which none of these men ever served. In March 1928, Liddell Hart wrote that the editors had rejected it. In person, Mrs. Fuller accused Liddell Hart of treating her husband "shabbily." Liddell Hart wrote to refute that accusation and prior accusations of plagiarism and ingratitude.

> I find somewhat tiring the suggestion that your qualities are not properly appreciated by myself – who have actually recognized them more fully and done more to proclaim them than anybody else. And I dislike the dissemination of the idea that my supposed attitude is ill-repayment to one who "helped me up the first rungs of the ladder." Here my dislike is mainly due to my objection to legends. Our friendship ought to be able to stand the strain of truth. Thus it may serve a useful purpose to deal with the first suggestion and also to put on record the facts of our relationship as I see them, so that you can confirm them. If you are the big man [that] I believe you to be, this frankness will clear the air for good…
>
> Whether any of my efforts on your behalf have been fruitful or not I cannot judge. In any case I am not claiming any gratitude, because they were not inspired by mere friendship but by my belief in your qualities. At the same time it is a fact, which I imagine you will admit, that both in print and in talk I have paid infinitely more and higher tributes to you than vice versa. Don't think I complain of your failure in this respect, for I know that you have a high opinion of hardly anyone. And I prefer sincerity. It is a further fact that my support of you has frequently been a cause of estrangement with other people and a handicap to my success, whereas by agreeing with or avoiding controversy when you have been

assailed, I could have won easy popularity, and advantaged by own prestige. Here again don't imagine I regret my attitude or claim any return. But to put this fact on record may help to prevent the absurdity of jealousy or rivalry ever creeping into our relations.

In the eyes of the Army and the public we are the two chief advocates of mechanization. When this comes about, origins may be obscured. So I will put on record this fact, lest others forget, that you were the pioneer and that my conversion did not begin till 1918 and was not complete till 1921. Up to that time I was essentially a pioneer in the field of infantry tactics and had hardly studied mechanical warfare (to Fuller, 11 March 1928, LHCMA LH 1/302).

Fuller confirmed their agreement on mechanization in general, but little else:

What an epistle, surely this is a storm in a teacup. I don't think I am jealous of you, or even that we are rivals. I welcome criticism of myself, but generally take little notice of it, and I have always valued your support. I do not pose as your master in any way, whether I have led you towards mechanization I do not know. Perhaps a little when we first met, now you are on your own...

Surely in ideas, anyhow on war, we are, if I may say so, partners not rivals. Partners, not actually working in collaboration, but towards the same goal (i.e. "The Remaking of Modern Armies" [1927b]) by the roads which suit our fancies best. To attempt to work otherwise would be, I feel, impossible, for we are both individualists. As a matter of fact[,] in detail there is very little in common in our respective work (to LH, 14 March and 3 April 1928, LHCMA LH 1/302).

In the following year, Liddell Hart published his debt to Fuller. Later, he and his followers ignored this publication. It disproves his countless claims that Fuller prescribed an "all-tank" army, while he prescribed mechanized combined arms.

[Fuller] prophesied and advocated the complete mechanization of armies, and proclaimed the abdication of infantry – the former "queen of battles."

At first[,] he was contemptuously dismissed as a mere crank and made few converts. Perhaps I was one of the earliest – at least in open acceptance. Constant debate between us had drawn me over to his side and, somewhat ironically, the final stage of my conversion came when, as a presumed authority on infantry, I was asked to expound the case against mechanization. The best arguments I could find failed to convince one reader – myself.

Henceforth I joined with "Boney" Fuller in leading the advocacy of mechanization, and the fact of my "infantry" predilection being known may have added some value to the reinforcement. The campaign for the new infantry doctrine was complete; the campaign for a doctrine of mechanized warfare now developed (1929c: 97).

Martel (1931: ix) began his history of the first fifteen years of mechanization by noting that public "interest was roused mainly by Major-General JFC Fuller, who wrote profusely and in a most attractive manner on the subject for many years after the war." Fuller (1932: 1; 1943: 2) promised, and warned, that mechanization offers "the greatest revolution that has ever taken place in the history of land warfare." Subsequently, Liddell Hart added a credit "to General Fuller's fertilizing ideas," in "thought and experiment" (1935: 155). However, he deleted Fuller from credit for his own conversion from pedestrianism to "the inevitability of mechanization."

> My own definite acceptance of the inevitability of mechanization – and perception of the advantage of taking the lead – dates from 1921. Then, as the author of the post-war Infantry Training [manual] [of which he actually authored only two pages], and of various unofficial treatises on infantry tactics, I was asked to take up the challenge that the tank offered and draft the case against mechanization [in fact, General Ivor Maxse asked for a draft entry entitled "Infantry" for the Encyclopaedia Britannica, under Maxse's name]. The arguments I found seemed to satisfy those who read my paper. But they failed to satisfy me. And from that moment I was forced, in honesty, to do my best to make clear the case for mechanization (1935: 297).

Unlike Liddell Hart, Fuller disliked public attention, intellectual conflict, and self-promotion; he remained a full-time soldier and thus subject to censorship; and he did not yet archive his correspondence or notes (Bond 1977: 220).

After Fuller died, Liddell Hart denigrated Fuller as caustic, isolated, and tank-obsessed (1965: II, 40, 42, 51), and claimed that "there were few contributors to the theme and theory of armoured warfare [other than myself]" (1965: I, 269).

Anthony Trythall found otherwise. "In 1920 Fuller was the more original and it was he who in a sense educated Liddell Hart and helped his individual genius to flower" (1977: 92-93). Shelford Bidwell found both of them impractical.

> Even Liddell Hart and Fuller, the two best minds who have attacked the problems of warfare, did not really understand the technology of modern weapons, the consequences of their interaction and the philosophy behind them; everything they wrote revealed they were obsessed by strategy, and saw the tank as a constant, immutable factor...
>
> Fuller infected him with enthusiasm for the tank and for mobile mechanized warfare, [while Charles] Broad gave him his early ideas on armoured strategy (Bidwell 1973: 51, 194).

Brian Bond (1977: 27) admits that "Liddell Hart's complete conversion to the opinion that tanks would constitute the decisive weapon in future warfare stemmed mainly from his association with Colonel JFC Fuller, which began in 1920." Bond and Alexander (1986: 601) admit that "Fuller was the bolder, more dynamic, and original thinker; Liddell Hart was more balanced, tactful, and less extravagant as a military polemicist." These are accurate statements. Yet Bond and Alexander invent two false "differences between the pioneers' thinking on mechanization." First, Liddell Hart advanced "more detailed and realistic plans" for a "New Model Army." Second, Liddell Hart advanced more mechanized infantry.

John Mearsheimer (1988: 206) found that "Liddell Hart owed a great intellectual debt to Fuller, one he never publicly acknowledged." Brian Holden Reid (1987: 161) too found that Fuller was necessary to Liddell Hart's intellectual development. Alex Danchev (1998: 115) agreed that "Fuller was a godsend. Here was someone he could neither out-argue nor out-think, truly a superior intellectual being…At the fag-end of his Army career Liddell Hart needed all the intoxication he could get." Azar Gat (1998: 184) admitted Fuller's influence on Liddell Hart's doctrines and policies, but nevertheless claimed that "Liddell Hart has not been given sufficient credit as their pioneer." A reviewer of Danchev, Reid, and Gat, "conclude[d]…that the great intellectual debt which Liddell Hart owed to Fuller has been until recently woefully underestimated" (Searle 2001: 347).

Neither Fuller nor Liddell Hart were sufficiently interested in the technologies to make practical their rather abstract theories. At least Fuller had experience with tanks, and had seen his own official requirements processed as procurements and acquisitions. By contrast, Liddell Hart had no experience with tanks, and, worse, took surprisingly little interest in their technologies, preferring convenient assumptions, as explained in the next chapter.

Fuller first specified a medium tank in April 1918. The Medium D Modified (D.M.) was the last medium evolved from wartime designs. Indeed, design work dates from May. It satisfies the weight (18-20 long tons), speed (20 mph), and range (150 miles) that Fuller had specified, and his additional specification of amphibiousness, but fell short in size, reliability, stability, and armor (12 mm). This first pilot was photographed upon first run in 1921, without armaments or cupolas. Fuller specified three machine-guns (Female) or one six-pounder gun and two machine-guns (Male), and four crewmen. Its designer (Colonel Philip Johnson) prioritized speed, so he reduced the fighting compartment, pushed it forward, and never installed armaments. To the same end, Johnson conceived and designed the track suspension, and uprated the automotive parts, so none of his products ever satisfied the specified reliability (1,000 miles between failures). Johnson subsequently drew versions closer to Fuller's wishes, including a turreted Male, but his department was deleted in 1923. This is when Liddell Hart made contact, contributing to his mania for speed (LHCMA LH 9/28/104-111 and 119-120; Fuller 1920: 45-47).

CHAPTER 3

Tank Technologies

Liddell Hart enjoyed privileged access to Fuller and Martel by the mid-1920s, and worthily supported mechanization in general and tanks in particular, but took little interest in the technologies. This was a life-long problem, as best evidenced by his misunderstandings of tracked transport, disinterest in the tanks of the Great War, unreliable automotive observations, and vain claims about communications.

Tracked Transport

Liddell Hart's first articles advocate for tracked transport for off-road logistics (1919b: 668), but overestimate tracked speed and efficiency. Liddell Hart's switch from pedestrianism to mechanization was slow and uncertain, despite Fuller's enthusiasm. He developed his next articles slowly, while he rebutted criticisms of his pedestrian "man-in-the-dark," "expanding torrent," and "contracting funnel" doctrines. Here his only use of the word "tank" is within his requirement for a "supply tank" to carry each infantry platoon's equipment and supplies (1922e: 304). In a concurrent article, he prospects unarmored, unarmed "mechanical transport" to carry infantry up to the battlefield, pending acquisition of some sort of armed, armored, tracked carrier (mistermed "tank") to carry each infantry section/squad (then about seven men) (1922d: 288).

His full conversion to Fuller's vision of a small, all-mechanized offensive force unfortunately carries forward his misimpressions that tracked vehicles in general are faster, more efficient, and less wearing than wheeled vehicles.

> On roads that have been cut up or are little better than tracks, the caterpillar vehicle scores in speed every time over the wheeled vehicle. In the next place, the roads, of Europe particularly, are far from level, considered as a whole. On gradients, the caterpillar machine with the new sprung track is actually faster than the wheeled vehicle of equal horsepower; the feet of the track grip the surface better than the wheel, and have the further advantage that they damage the surface less – a factor of immense importance, not only for war but also for peace purposes.
>
> Therefore, for the conveyance of loads the use of the caterpillar lorry is better economy of force than that of the wheeled lorry, for its margin of superiority on poor surfaces is immense, whilst on good surfaces, except in flat country, its lesser speed in proportion to power output on the level is balanced by its greater speed per horsepower in undulating country. The principle of economy of force tells us that a vehicle which has a definite commercial value has a decided advantage from a military standpoint, as its chances of mechanical development are greater and its expansion in emergency assured.

> For surprise, the fact that the caterpillar vehicle can move off the roads defeats the enemy's information and establishes its superiority over the wheeled vehicle, which is of necessity tied to the arteries of traffic – these are shown on the map and can be kept under observation from the air.
>
> In concentration, the caterpillar machine solves the problem of congestion which has always been the brake on concentration of force at the decisive point.
>
> It is not suggested that roads will be abandoned – so long as good roads exist it is more advantageous to use a smooth surface than a broken one. But the chain-track does enable the concentration of traffic on any particular line of movement to be multiplied, not merely double or quadruple, but tenfold, twenty-fold, or even more (1924a: 95).

Writing in the same year, he makes a mechanical analogy to economics that betrays misunderstandings of both mechanics and economics.

> Just as the engine and transmission of an automobile, because of the intricacy and delicacy of their joints and working parts, are far more susceptible to damage than the road wheels, so in a modern nation at war its industrial resources and communications form its Achilles' heel (1925: 34).

Even his use of the semantic frame "mechanical" is unreliable. Writing in 1934, he claims to see "a widening attempt to develop minds capable of the masterful use of mechanical weapons." Here, his "mechanical weapons" are experimental light infantrymen, moving on foot and in rough terrain, in order to avoid real mechanical weapons (1935: 233).

Great War Tanks

Liddell Hart's book on the "Decisive Wars of History" mentions tanks only three times: once to praise British use of tanks instead of a preliminary bombardment at Cambrai (20 November 1917); once to praise French use of light tanks; and once to note greater Allied use of tanks at Amiens (8 August 1918). On a draft, T.E. Lawrence (Lawrence of Arabia) wrote: "Tactically, of course, our victory was spelt TANKS." Liddell Hart ignored this observation (1929a: 175, 222, 223; 1938b: 21).

His book-length history of the Great War addresses tanks across less than nine of its 464 pages of main body text. One chapter is a review of the development of the first British heavy tank. It indulges his prejudice against military conservatism, and thence praises Winston Churchill's triumph over this conservatism. He misdescribes the tank as "evolved" from Benjamin Holt's "agricultural tractor," and misreports a "lack of any exact specification of the military requirements" (1930b: 250, 254; 1936a). In fact, Churchill had hidden his landship projects from the War Office, until he was removed from direction of the Admiralty. The Holt tractor and the landships projects were not necessary to the eventual tank, which was specified, designed, and developed by soldiers and civilian partners, without the Admiralty (Newsome 2021a: chapter 1).

In trying to prove soldierly conservativism towards tanks, he offers hearsay as if personal observation.

> [O]ne recalls Mr. L.E. de Mole's model, superior to the 1916 tank, which was pigeonholed in the War Office in 1912. To these add also the story of the Nottingham plumber whose hobby it was to make toy machines of this nature, and whose design, submitted to the War Office in 1911, and duly pigeonholed, was unearthed after the war, the file bearing the terse official comment, "The man's mad" (1930b: 252).

Within years, he conflates the two stories into one story.

> After the last war the plans of a tank, designed in 1912 and more advanced than the actual machine of 1916, were unearthed from the dusty recesses of the British War Office and found to bear this brief verdict of authority – "The man's mad" (1932c: 123-124; 1935: 116).

Liddell Hart's histories of the Great War have nothing to say about the employment of tanks, except to complain that Douglas Haig (commander of the BEF) was too eager to use the first batch of tanks (in September 1916) – which contradicts his complaint about conservatism. He states that at Messines (June 1917) "the effect of the mines [explosive tunnels] and artillery was so overwhelming that the tanks were hardly needed." He attributes the break-in at Cambrai (November 1917) to "surprise and the tank," but ultimately just "surprise." This contrasts with his other comment that "[t]he only close approach to a breakthrough by the British had been at Cambrai, with the tanks." The book's conclusions are platitudinous and evasive. The tank became "a greater landmark in the history of the war than in the history of the Somme, so it is likely to become a still greater landmark in the history of war." On the last page he lists "the tank" as one of many things whose contribution to victory would be "futile" to assess (1930b: 245, 249, 251, 258, 303, 332, 356, 390, 476; 1934: 254, 256, 464).

In his fourth and final history of the Great War, he complains about British use of tanks in too few numbers (September 1916), in "mass" on "dry" land but without "reserves" (November 1917), and in "great mass" (August 1918). Yet he claims that the few German tanks broke the British line wherever they were "introduced," which seems like another attempt to prove British military conservatism. Tanks do not appear in the conclusion or the index (1938a: 17, 20, 23, 288).

During the 1950s, he led the official history of the British tank arm. The chapters covering the Great War were written by several unnamed current tank officers – all of them relying on Fuller's first history of the tank arm (1920). Correlli Barnett was then a budding historian who enquired about the chapters.

> I once had a correspondence with him about the development of tanks in the Great War[,] and he did not seem to be aware of the enormous difficulties in actually developing the tank[,] and he ascribed the slowness of the tank to come to the field to the obstruction of the War Office and the Generals – but in fact it was because of the technical difficulties of producing the tank in the factories, casting the track links, supplying a workable engine, things of this kind (in Howard 1979: 27).

Automotive Technologies

Liddell Hart liked expensive cars, and portrayed himself as a good driver and mechanic, but a motorist is not necessarily a mechanic. He probably never looked in the engine compartment of any vehicle. His son doubted that he ever entered a tank, even though he arranged for the son to take rides in tanks during summer maneuvers (Adrian Liddell Hart 1953: 19; Danchev 1998: 6, 31). He once equated the ride of a tankette off road to a car on road (1932c: 179), unwittingly proving that he had never ridden a tankette either.

The practice that best reveals the unreliability of Liddell Hart's automotive observations is his repeated claim to clock the speed of Vickers Medium tanks. He was actually observing his own car's speedometer, as he followed tanks, during the Army's summer maneuvers, around tight public roads in the countryside of south-eastern England. He reported their top speed as sometimes 30 mph, sometimes 25 mph. Writing in 1931, he describes a "speed of about 20 miles an hour." The latter is closest to the truth. In fact, the latest Medium Mark II reached 18 mph in official tests. A record 21.5 mph was achieved on 9 June 1936 by an under-loaded Mark II, downhill on the hard road known as the "flying quarter-mile," at the Mechanical Experimental Establishment – a site he never visited (1932c: 126; 1935: 113; to Ogorkiewicz, 11 February 1957, RACTM E2015.2015.64; 1965: I, 95; MEE, 1936, RACTM E2006.1453; Ross 1976: 115).

His selection bias towards British Army conservatism provoked him to misrepresent tank "maintenance stops" (to check fluids and for damage, every 30 minutes on the march) as tactical relegation "behind the infantry," as if automobiles were being tied to pedestrian pace. Hypocritically, the following paragraph characterizes soldiers as less technically interested.

> The hardest problem today is not so much to obtain better machines as to obtain officers trained to think "mechanically." Perhaps we shall never obtain them unless we either go to the London General Omnibus Company and Pickfords to provide our strategists and staff in another war, or send our rising officers to such organizations for training (1932c: 217; 1935: 191).

Here he betrays his ignorance of current mechanical training. All ranks of the Tank Corps, the Royal Army Service Corps, and the Royal Army Ordnance Corps received mechanical training. Students of the Advanced Course at the Military College of Science (an alternative to Staff College, intended for officer technicians, designers, and acquirers) seconded students to private suppliers and users, including the London General Omnibus Company.

In the 1950s, Richard Ogorkiewicz made contact, a young automotive engineer in search of sources and jobs. He became Liddell Hart favorite unpaid researcher of tank specifications. Ogorkiewicz recalled that "Liddell Hart was a keen motorist," who used his motoring to inform his thinking about tanks, but otherwise took no interest in technologies.

> [Liddell Hart] was certainly more inclined to think of them in terms of mobility than fighting capabilities. To be fair, in one of his early papers he wrote of tanks armed with powerful guns (of 120mm if I remember correctly)[*] [actually a self-propelled 6-inch howitzer] but in general he did

---

[*] Ogorkiewicz here paraphrases Liddell Hart's letter about the article (11 February 1954, RACTM E2015.2015.62), not the article (1924c), which he probably never read.

not seem very interested in their fighting capabilities…But, like others around him, he was more interested in the automotive performance of armoured vehicles and their strategic or tactical capabilities than in their technology. So, to my knowledge, he did not collect information about the detailed, technical characteristics of tanks (to author, 25 July 2016).

Brian Bond, who knew them both from 1958, recalled that "Liddell Hart was notoriously unmechanical and impractical" (2015: 36).

Signals and Communications

The first British tanks used flags, semaphore, visual panels, smoke, and pigeons to communicate in battle, and used telephone cable at rest. Radios then were larger and heavier than telephone sets. Still, radios were used in tanks tactically from July 1917. Liddell Hart misreported that "General Headquarters would not allow the [radio] equipment to be sent out, and it was dispersed" (1930b: 258).

The Tank Corps and Royals Signals Corps started trying specialist radios for tanks from the mid-1920s. Those radios were supplied by the Signals Experimental Establishment, in cooperation with the Superintendent of Design's tank section, after years of development. They went through about a dozen models by World War II. Liddell Hart knew, because he reported (in journalism and books) on Charles Broad's use of radios in command tanks in the temporary tank brigades of 1929 and 1931, and Percy Hobart's use of the same in the permanent Tank Brigade from 1934 (1932c: 204-205, 247; 1935: 178-179, 212, 221, 282; 1960: 189-190).

Yet Liddell Hart never mentioned the authorities, probably because to credit them would discredit his claims of military conservatism. After the Second World War, Hobart summarized the history of tank radios for Liddell Hart's official history of the tank arm (which Hobart was managing). Hobart makes clear that his historical inspirations for wireless command and control were "the Tartars and Cromwell's cavalry" (Hobart to LH, "Wireless," 1948, LHCMA LH 1/376/7). Nevertheless, after Hobart's death, Liddell Hart's memoirs claim that Hobart was inspired by "my account of the Mongol campaigns and forces, which emphasized how much their effectiveness had depended on solving the problem of control" (1965: I, 248). In fact, his first publication on Mongols remarks on "their [tactical] evolutions carried out by signals with the black-and-white flags of the squadrons," without drawing any lessons for radios (1924b: 656). His subsequent writings on the Mongols emphasize "mobility," without mentioning the problem of control (1927c: 22; 1932c: 257; 1935: 65; 1950: 221; 1965: I, 166). The British Army standardized tank radios 15 years after he first published on the Mongols, once the radios were technologically mature. They were not historically inspired.

Liddell Hart's inattentiveness to technologies was convenient to his enthusiasm for faster, lighter vehicles that could fulfill his hope for shorter wars and thence less costly wars – indeed for wars without fighting. This explains his unwavering opposition to heavy tanks, as explained in the next chapter.

CHAPTER 4

Heavy Tanks

The first British and French tanks to be deployed (in 1916) were classed as "heavy." British heavies weighed less than 30 metric tons (29.5 long; 33.1 short), including the preferred wartime and peacetime model (Mark V). The latest evoluations (produced in 1918 but not deployed) approached 40 tons. British, French, and German designs included super-heavy tanks that would have weighed hundreds of tons. British mediums started at 14 tons, and approached 20 tons in their latest variants. French, American, and Italian light tanks weighed less than 7 tons.

Liddell Hart wanted lighter still. Liddell Hart's writings do not specify any weight classes, until he compares the British Army's *Field Service Regulations* with the French equivalent. Here he realizes French "light tanks." In his discussion of the characteristics of the different arms, the only notable point of difference is that in the French manual the tanks are dealt with under the heading "infantry" and are treated solely as infantry supports. He is happy with this role. He would not raise any independent raiding role for another decade (1922f: 667-668).

In a subsequent article, he admits heavy tanks, but misunderstands French doctrine.

> ...a first echelon of heavy tanks, armed with an armour-piercing gun or light howitzer, to advance before the infantry deployment and clear the way of hostile tanks and anti-tank forts; and a second echelon of light tanks, armed with machine-guns and possibly mortars, to be launched concurrently or just subsequent to the infantry deployment...concentrating on the destruction of centres of resistance which trouble the infantry (1924c: 43).

By then, the British Army was replacing legacy heavy tanks with new light tanks. The Army's first tank of both peacetime design and mass-production was then designated as the Vickers Light Tank Mark I (piloted 1923, issued 1924). It weighed barely 11 long tons (12.3 short). The latest versions weighed less than 12 long tons (13.4 short) when reclassified as Mediums (in 1927). Liddell Hart wanted lighter. Like Fuller, Liddell Hart doubted "that we shall see land 'Dreadnoughts'" or "land ships," given "obstacles and surface friction" and "damage to property." The capacity of roads and bridges alone "will limit the size of the landships." "[T]he novelists' dream of land dreadnoughts is unlikely of fruition." Unlike Fuller, he did not see heavy tanks as complementary to light tanks, but rather as drags on the speed of every platform (1924c: 44; 1925: 81).

Tenuously, he used self-propelled artillery to justify light tanks, as if artillery by indirect fire could neutralize anything that light tanks could not handle by direct fire (he wanted nothing heavier than a medium machine-gun in a light tank). The British Army had deployed tracked self-propelled 5-inch 60-pounder guns and 6-inch howitzers from 1917 to 1918, and already required a tracked self-propelled

(Below) The Mark V Male was delivered in 1918 with a six-pounder gun at front of each sponson, a machine-gun at rear of same, and another for a ball mounting at each end. (Right) Birch Gun Mark Ib, the second in a batch of four vehicles delivered in 1926.

18-pounder field gun on the Vickers Medium Mark II platform ("Birch Gun"). He requires a minority of field guns to be "mounted permanently on caterpillar transports with collapsible armour-plated all-round protection." He wants howitzers (unspecified) to be mounted similarly. He calls them "tanks," even though wartime self-propelled artillery had been officially classified as "Gun Carriers" (given that the preferred firing platform was the ground). He relegates towed "heavy artillery" to bombardment of fortifications, given his mistaken belief that aircraft "hit a moving target with greater accuracy." He prioritizes light tanks, but his specifications are closer to the recently canceled Medium D.M. He specifies a "tank of the modern type" with the armor and speed of a light tank (28 to 30 mph on road, 15-20 mph across country), but the armament of a Mark V "Hermaphrodite" or "Composite" ("one six-pounder gun and three light automatics") (1924a: 41, 100).

In his plan, the Tank Corps would receive mostly self-propelled field guns and howitzers. The true proportion is confused by his conflation of "tank" with gun carriers and self-propelled firing platforms. He never specifies guns in turrets (as in current light tanks), ball-mountings (as in current medium tanks), sponsons (as in current heavy tanks), open platforms (as in the Birch Gun), or dismountable carriages (as in the deleted 60-pounder Gun Carrier Mark I).

He proposes an interim division with a company of "divisional cavalry," a battalion of "pursuit tanks," three battalions of Vickers Light/Medium Mark I tanks, three units of self-propelled 18-pounders or 4.5-inch howitzers – presumably for direct fire (mistermed as "heavy tanks"), and three units of self-propelled 18- to 60-pounder guns – presumably for indirect fire. His proposed terminal division ("New Model Division") would hold a battalion of "light and very fast scout tanks of, say 6-8 tons, armed with machine-guns and armoured over the vitals only," six battalions of "fast cruiser tanks of about 20 tons, well-armoured and with an armour-piercing gun as primary armament," three units of self-propelled artillery or assault guns (mistermed as "heavy battle tanks") – each vehicle weighing "35-50 tons, carrying one or more 60-p[ounde]rs or 6-inch howitzers, sacrificing some degree of speed to gun-power and protection," and one unit of "gas projecting tanks" (1924c: 43, 45).*

In 1926, he conflates "artillery tanks" and "battleship tanks." He does not define or specify them, but they seem to be the heaviest possible self-propelled artillery. His only other AFVs in this particular writing are tankettes.

In the same year, the British Army demonstrated the 33-ton Vickers "Independent," as a heavy tank, but Liddell Hart did not report it at the time. Later in the year, after the Army had revealed an official requirement for a heavier medium tank, Liddell Hart suddenly dismisses the Vickers Light/Medium tank as "an interim and an expensive weapon," and requires "a larger tank, strongly armoured and with a heavier armament." He contradicts himself by dismissing the Experimental Mechanized Force (EMF) of that summer in favor of the "old lightness and mobility" (1927a: 80).

After the Second World War, Liddell Hart misrepresented the self-propelled artillery in his article as "heavy tanks," with larger tank guns than Fuller had wanted. He published the same in his memoirs, except to admit that Fuller had warned of the article's "chilly reception." In fact, Fuller always required armored self-propelled artillery, primarily for indirect fire. Fuller required higher-velocity versions of the 3-pounder tank gun (in the current Light Tank Mark I) and six-pounder tank gun (in current Heavy tanks), primarily as anti-tank guns, but with a sufficiently destructive shell so that the assault/heavy and close-support types of tank could be hybridized. Fuller specified also a "heavy machine-gun" of 0.5-inch or 1.0-inch calibre, for anti-personnel use. Liddell Hart ignored heavy machine-guns then, but later would place them as towed anti-tank guns (Fuller 1926: 367; LH to Ogorkiewicz, 11 February 1954, RACTM E2015.2015.62; 1965: I, 92).

By the late 1920s, Liddell Hart abandons self-propelled artillery. He now imagines that tankettes and bombers, thanks to speed, can target anything, anywhere, without need for indirect fire. In the interim, before full reliance on bombers, he allows "heavy tractor-drawn artillery, which, like the siege engines of antiquity, will be brought up only when the enemy is found in a fortified position." He mischaracterizes bombers as "the most effective and economic means of long-range bombardment." The largest direct-fire piece he would allow is "a 3-pounder or, at most, 6-pounder gun," on something no larger than the current Vickers Light/Medium tank. He would delete the 18-pounder field gun, on two grounds: its ammunition is too light to affect entrenchments; and its carriage is too slow, even when pulled by automobiles. Of course, this does not explain why he does not require larger guns on faster self-propelled carriages (1932c: 132-133; 1935: 118-119).

He characterizes the "offensive value" of French "heavy guns and tanks" (each less than 25 tons currently) as "limited against any army with adequate machine-

---

* The article is unclear whether the New Model Division would include the interim division's three units of self-propelled 18-pounders and 60-pounders. In a concurrent book, he allows for no "field artillery" other than what can be "fitted in a tank," if they are to survive aircraft and tanks (1925: 69).

A Char 2C delivered in 1921. The Vickers Independent in 1926.

guns" (1932c: 171; 1935: 157). He contradicts himself, where he admits that French heavies (with armor up to 25-mm thick) and super-heavies (45-mm) are immune from the same armor-piercing bullets that could defeat the Vickers Light/Medium (1932c: 176). Yet he imagines that larger tanks can be destroyed by machine-guns, and would be useless if infantry "had time to dig themselves into narrow trench-slits" and "were well dispersed and 'lay doggo'" (1932c: 234-235; 1935: 208-209).

> After the war, most armies, under French influence, persevered with the heavily armoured type of tank which, being sluggish, was intended merely as a direct aid to the infantry in attack. The British, however, developed a new fast type, lightly armoured and capable of a speed of about 20 miles an hour…
>
> In the last year or two, the diverging lines of French and British tank design have shown some sign of converging anew, the French giving increased speed both to their small tanks and to their super-heavy 70-ton tanks [Char 2C of 1921], while the British have added somewhat thicker armour, as well as a fresh increase of speed in the 30- [33-ton Vickers "Independent" of 1926] and 16-ton [A6 of 1928] tanks which have followed the original fast 11-ton tank of 1923, still their standard machine.
>
> The French 70-ton tank, which carries armour no less than 55 [actually: 45] millimeters thick, naturally suggests the idea of future land dreadnoughts. But such speculations fail to take account of the difficulties imposed by rivers, railways, and other obstacles. There are few bridges which could bear so heavy a machine without collapsing. For a specialized purpose, such as that of breaking through a strongly entrenched line, this moving fortress might have value. For general utility, I doubt whether such large machines have a future. The bigger the machine the bigger the target, and on land the gun has far greater advantages in its competition with armour than at sea. It would not be easy to produce a tank with armour thick enough to resist a direct hit from modern field artillery, whilst the larger such machines become the more exposed they are to air-bombing. In any case, the high cost of these super-heavy tanks makes their development impossible, save experimentally, in peace time (1932c: 127-128; 1935: 113-114).

He follows the passage above with a characterization of "the miniature tank" as "a more promising line of tank development." He had already abandoned "tanks" in favor of "tankettes" – which continue to confuse his readers, thanks to his careless use of terms. Tankettes are the subject of the next chapter.

CHAPTER 5

Tankettes and Carriers

From 1920, the government's design and production authorities experimented with small, tracked carriers, tractors, and tanks. In August 1921, the General Staff required a fully-tracked armored carrier for a heavy (0.5-inch) machine-gun, to be dismounted before firing, as an anti-tank weapon. The CIGS ruled that the design should provide for firing from the vehicle. The Tank Corps' preference was for all tanks to be armed with larger guns. This became consensual policy in March 1922, during specification of an anti-tank vehicle that would become the Vickers Light Tank Mark I (DCIGS, "Tank and Anti-Tank Design," 29 August and 6 September 1921, RACTM E1963.46.10-11; Hugh Elles, 17 March 1922, RACTM E1963.46.9).

Official preferences for anti-tank guns and turrets (a turret differentiates a tank from a carrier) likely explain Liddell Hart's subsequent remark: "The conversion of armies into pure tank force is likely to be delayed by many causes – not least by the inertia of conservatism." Here he is comparing British doctrine harshly against the latest French manual. He welcomes the latter's requirement for lighter infantry and machine-guns. The French manual's introduction, he reports, "speculates on the question whether this evolution will eventually terminate in two or three men enclosed in an armoured and mobile shell" (1922a: 233, 237).

Soon, Liddell Hart fancies that smaller AFVs combine equestran speed over open country with pedestrian mobility and vision in close country:

> A small and light chain-tracked machine could be produced even now which would move over any kind of ground traversable by cavalry, except dense woods and hill tracks. If the general mobility of such a machine is greater than that of the cavalryman[,] and the loco-mobility of the man on foot is similarly greater than that of the cavalryman, the deduction is surely that the sum of the two is greater. Any reconnaissance, therefore, could surely be carried out far quicker, and with at least equal results, by a chain-tracked machine, whose crew could leave their machine when necessary and carry out the detailed exploration on foot, than by the cavalryman. Moreover the need of the latter for a horse-holder when he dismounts for reconnaissance over very broken ground infringed the principle of economy of force (1924a: 99-100).

His fancy relies too much on Medieval Mongolian warfare.

> [T]he armoured caterpillar car or light tank appears the natural heir of the Mongol horseman, for the "caterpillars" are essentially mechanical cavalry. Reflection suggests that we might well regain the Mongol mobility and offensive power by reverting to the simplicity of a single highly mobile arm, employing the crews to act on foot as land marines wherever the special loco-mobility of infantry is needed (1924b: 658-659).

He prospects masses of small, light, bullet-proof "tanks," given his mistaken expectation that the "chances" of a hit from aircraft and artillery "would be infinitely less against a modern tank zigzagging at over 20 mph, and infinitesimal against them if launched in masses" (1925: 69). He seems to be biased by his nervousness around current Vickers light/medium tanks:

Martel demonstrates his "One-Man Tank" in August 1925.

> To anyone who has experienced the sense of helplessness caused by the sight of the modern tanks racing towards one at 20 mph, sweeping over banks and nullahs, swinging [a]round with amazing agility in their own length, the question arises: "Can flesh and blood, however heroic, be persuaded to face them?" It is a sight to freeze the blood of a witness with imagination to grasp the demoralizing effect if their guns and machine-guns were actually spitting forth death (1925:70).

In July 1925, two months after this comment was published, Martel invited him to see a vehicle that Martel was fabricating in his garage. The design accommodates one man within a proud metal box, to the rear of the compartment for the engine, on a chassis with two wheels at the rear and tracks at the front. The box was cut with a slit for a notional light machine-gun. Martel, his eventual partners, and their competitors marketed this class as "Small Tank," but the British Army categorized it as "tankette." By Martel's own account, only Liddell Hart and a second-class General Staff Office (GSO2) (Major Pierse Joseph Mackesy) supported the vehicle. Back in January, Martel had prospected a "small tank" to a separate staff officer in the DMO&I (Major Henry Karslake), probably because Karslake had proposed "light machine-gun tanks" in 1919. Karslake invited Martel to submit a proposal. Karslake's invitation was probably casual. He was a few months away from leaving DMO&I for a staff position at Southern Command HQ. His Director (John Burnett-Stuart) did not record any such proposal in his papers (Martel 1927: 59; Martel 1931: 110; Martel 1949: 51; Liddell Hart 1965: I, 123).

During Liddell Hart's first visit, he and Martel plotted a journalistic report to market the vehicle. They claimed that tankettes are as lethal as tanks (in fact, the current Vickers Light/Medium mounts a 3-pounder gun and multiple machine-guns), could go where the current arms could not (in fact, their obstacle-crossing capabilities are inferior), could swarm but not be targeted (in fact, their only advantage over tanks is portability), and offer the same capabilities for less cost (in fact, the turret – the most expensive of the tank's differentiations – enhances lethality, ergonomics, and survivability). Portability and cheapness fulfill popular cultural and political imperatives for cost efficiencies and ready deployment, but the Army still required an anti-tank tank.

Liddell Hart's first report on Martel's "One-Man Tank" appeared in *The Daily Telegraph* on 28 August, days after Martel demonstrated it on a nearby heath, to journalists and officials. Martel read the report that evening, with regret. Fuller, who had been among the officials, and judged the vehicle useless, telephoned that evening to express "surprise and annoyance." Martel admitted fault to Fuller, over the telephone and by letter, but felt bullish by the time he wrote to Liddell Hart:

At first I feared you had gone rather beyond our agreement, but on reading it through again I see that nothing is given away. I am not out for any personal publicity so long as we can get them to make a move. I suggest it should be left quiet for a bit now, to see if they really get busy with it (to LH, 28 August 1925, LHCMA LH 1/492 Part 1).

The "Three-Man Tank" (project A3E1) in 1926

Liddell Hart did not stay quiet. By October, Martel acquiesced:

[A] lot of people, who do not normally read The Daily Telegraph, made a point of getting hold of it at the clubs to read your articles and to discuss them (to LH, 17 October 1925, LHCMA LH 1/492 Part 1).

In November, Martel's vehicle was despatched to the Tank Testing Section at Farnborough, Hampshire. Its commander (Lieutenant Daniel Sheryer, a tank officer and mechanical engineer) had already seen Martel's demonstration:

Martel was a very ingenious man...I think we were all impressed at the man's effort in demonstrating the possibilities of the small tank, [but I] was never a protagonist of the small tank, [partly because] it couldn't carry enough men to make it an effective fighting unit on its own (interview of D.M.F. Sheryer by D.G. Lance, 1976, RACTM E1998.19).

Current policy was that any tank should be crewed by at least three men (driver, gunner, commander). Sheryer escalated his scepticism of the "small tank" to the Chief Inspector of Armaments (CIA), where he started a new job in January 1926. The Director of Mechanization (billeted as Director of Artillery II until December 1927) (Major-General Sydney Peck) agreed to order two vehicles for trial during the summer. They made a useful contrast to the War Department's own "Machine-Gun Carrier Number 1" (project A3E1), which is fully-enclosed and -tracked, and accommodates three men and two machine-guns (one in a turret at each end, which is why it was known as also "Tank Number 1" or "Three-Man Tank"). Since August this had been assembled by the Royal Ordnance Factory in Woolwich Arsenal, to a design evolved from the Light Dragon tractor by the Superintendent of Design (also in the Woolwich Arsenal) (Pile 1949: 29; Ross 1976: 111).[*]

Martel partnered with Morris Motors of Birmingham to develop a two-man "small tank," but could not squeeze in three men. By January 1926, the WD had ordered a pair each of the one-man and two-man offerings. Peck warned Martel to stop the publicity, but Martel told Liddell Hart of Peck's "foolish attitude," and promised a photograph of the two-man (Martel to LH, 11 January 1926, LHCMA LH 1/492 Part 1; Martel 1931: 114; Martel 1949: 51, 149; Liddell Hart 1965: I, 77-78). Liddell Hart released the photograph alongside a report in *The Daily Telegraph* (31 March 1926), a few days after A3E1 and the one-man tankettes arrived at the Tank Testing Section. He enthused about the tankette's cheapness, without dwelling on

---

[*] The WD had deleted the tank design section in 1923. It was recreated, as DDM, in 1931.

capabilities. He imagines 60,000 tankettes defeating a larger force. Martel's estimated cost (£500 each) looks low compared to Liddell Hart's estimates of future armored tracked platoon carriers (£1,500 to £2,000 each) and unarmored carriers (£750 each). Yet cheapness is not necessarily the same as cost-effectiveness. At cost per person carried, the tankette (£500) is at least ten times more expensive than his imagined platoon carrier (no more than £50 per rider). Further, his assertion that 60,000 tankettes (£30,000,000) are cheaper than any other ground maneuver force is ill-informed. In July 1929, the General Staff estimated the cost of building on current inventory to assemble three "armoured brigades" (450 medium tanks and about as many wheeled automobiles, current types) at £454,000. Liddell Hart's proposal is 66 times costlier. He could claim savings in sustainment, by abandoning tanks for tankettes, but not by a multiple of 66. For the same cost as 60,000 tankettes, the Army could acquire 6 to 7 further "armoured brigades" of the type proposed in 1929, or 6 to 7 "tank brigades" of the type proposed in 1935, or 4 to 5 mechanized infantry divisions of the type proposed in 1935 (1924c: 39, 42; "A6 and Medium Mark III: Brief Notes on Development," RACTM E2011.1519; Macready 1935: 4). Nevertheless, Liddell Hart revived his proposal of March 1926 throughout the 1930s.

Two Medium Mark II Tanks, a Morris-Martel two-man tankette, and a motorcycle of 5th Battalion RTC on Penham Down, Salisbury Plain, in 1927.

> [I] had argued on both military and economic grounds that such vehicles must form the main constituent part of any mechanized force or army. Both because by cheapness they made quantity possible, and because by quantity only could we assure that the inevitable accidents and losses of war should not reduce our hitting power to zero. Quantity of small machines is an additional insurance because it enables a far wider distribution of the risk through the dispersed and minute targets thus offered (1932c: 197; 1935: 171).

By contrast, after the Second World War, Liddell Hart would pretend that his army of tankettes was an interim step towards the New Model Division that he had plagiarized from Fuller in 1924. He would claim also that by 1925 he had realized that the New Model Division's vehicles would be too costly to acquire in peacetime. Conveniently, he would pretend that the primary reason for the Army's under-mechanization was under-funding. In fact, it was confusion about types to acquire, to which he contributed most, first in the press, later in official advice (to Ogorkiewicz, 17 and 27 August 1961, RACTM E2015,2015.68; 1959: I, 29, 275).

The A3E1 and Morris-Martel vehicles were demonstrated to the press in August 1926. Liddell Hart misreported that each could be used to carry an infantry platoon. Martel, to his credit, reminded Liddell Hart that neither could. Martel asserted Morris 6x4 one-ton trucks as the best carriers for infantry (and for the mechanized company of engineers that Martel was commanding) (to LH, 8 August 1926, LH 1/492 Part 1). Within days, Liddell Hart wrote a new article, recommending six-wheeled trucks for infantry and machine-gunners, tankettes for the cavalry, and tankettes and medium tanks for the Tank Corps.

> [The tankette is] a much lighter machine-gun tank or car, which will gain security from its dispersion, its mobility, and the numbers which its cheapness will make possible...[It is also] a cavalry or destroyer tank. The prototype of this second class may be the Martel-Morris tankette, or it may be a cross-country armoured car...And we must also realize that our object is not to produce a mere reconnaissance machine, but to replace the now paralyzed infantry...[A] battalion of 300 two-man tanks would swamp any defensive position in moving warfare (1927a: 80-82).

He coyly declares the current Morris-Martel two-man tankette as sufficient, without admitting that the British Army preferred Carden-Loyd's competitor (fully tracked and lower profile, for the same armament and crew). His allowance for competition with "a cross-country armoured car" is a sleight of hand: this is how the Army termed the cavalry's requirement for a half-tracked scout vehicle, for which the only current bid was the Morris-Martel two-man tankette. He added dishonest expectations that tankettes could hide and escape from bombing and toxic gas. In fact, only the A3E1 was designed with overhead cover (1927a: 80).

In September 1926, Liddell Hart included in his reports on French maneuvers an urging for the French to replace their two-man light tank (FT, by Renault, introduced in 1918) with a tankette. His only justification is speed. He seems ignorant of the light tank's superior obstacle-crossing, lethality, and armor. He does not mention the medium and heavy tanks that the French were trying. He does not challenge the French subordination of tanks to infantry. Instead, he criticizes the technology alone, and betrays misunderstandings of technology and doctrine. His contempt for the FT is contradicted by his praise for the Italian version (which he had seen in 1928). He describes the French tank as "painfully slow and unreliable," the Italian version as "similar but superior," "tried in the Alps, with considerable success," and "able to move when their tracks were nearly buried in the snow." His bias is best explained by Italian experimentation with tankettes, ahead of their import of Carden-Loyd carriers in 1929, copies of which would replace all Italian tanks until the Second World War (1932c: 171, 177; 1941: 83-91).

His book for the Summer of 1927 contains a chapter questioning "The Mounted Infantry of the Future?" He urges the conversion of infantry to tankettes, given that "the machine-gun is master of the modern battlefield." He imagines that tankettes would pay for themselves by enabling the cut of about one-third of the current 136 infantry battalions (1927b: 12).

Following the maneuvers of September 1927, Liddell Hart lobbied the General Staff for restructuring of forces and tactics around tankettes and a few light tanks. He quickly repackaged his letter as articles for *The Daily Telegraph* and *The Journal of the Royal United Services Institution* (RUSI).

> And the issue of dummy anti-tank machine-guns to infantry battalions proved that these were too cumbrous and immobile for men to handle, and that such weapons could only be effective on a mechanized mounting – in other words, that to counter a tank we need a tankette ("Army Training, 1927," The Daily Telegraph, 27 September 1927: 9; 1927e: 747).

His requirement to replace tank with tankette, and his conflation of them, provoked rebuttal. He blamed the Army's "oppression and helplessness" (1927a: 69). Yet he also cut the paragraph above from subsequent self-plagiarisms. He left the paragraphs endorsing Aldershot Command's ruling that "tanks" should lead the infantry against machine-guns (1927e: 748; 1932c: 188; 1935: 161-162). This appears to contradict his emerging prescription for all-tank raids, but, confusingly, he means that tankettes should lead infantry assaults, while mediums wait to occupy the objective, and light tanks raid in the enemy's rear. His confidence in tankettes in the assault is clearest in the following paragraph, which he republished most often.

> [T]he position of every anti-tank gun which opened against them would be smothered with a thick spray of aimed machine-gun fire from the tankettes. It is difficult to imagine any gun-crew functioning effectively when this heavy spray of aimed bullets is added to the "water-hosing" fire of the on-rushing tanks ("Army Training, 1927," Daily Telegraph, 27 September 1927: 9; 1927e: 752; 1932c: 193; 1935: 167-168; 1965: I, 178).

For the maneuvers of Summer 1928, eight Morris-Martel and eight Carden-Loyd vehicles were available. These were gathered in one company, within the "Fast Group" of the Experimental Armoured Force.

> [T]heir presence was not only of experimental but of argumentative value. For it was a reinforcement to those who contended that, as soon as the improved Carden-Loyds were available, the force should divest itself of its existing paraphernalia of Dragon-drawn field guns, self-propelled 18-pounders, lorry-borne 3.7[-inch] howitzers, and unarmoured machine-guns. This vulnerable miscellany hampered and complicated the speed, security, and handling of the force without equivalent compensation. It had, indeed, the air of a large chorus as a vocal background to the few unduly prominent stars. The performance led me, as one of the audience, to urge anew "that the fighting part of a true armoured force should be mainly composed of light tanks such as the new Carden-Loyd, with a proportion of 'gun tanks' such as the new 16-ton Vickers [A6] for its extra fire support, and perhaps a sprinkling of six-wheeled armoured cars as its long-range "feelers" (1932c: 197-198; 1935: 172).

By then, Liddell Hart was a fan of Carden-Loyd tankettes too. Initially, he had refused to give them publicity, but his advocacy for tankettes had inspired John Carden's partnership with Vivian Loyd in 1925. In September 1927, Liddell Hart observed Major Frederick "Tim" Pile manoeuvring his "Fast Group" of armored cars and Carden-Loyd tankettes. They started to correspond. In 1928, Pile joined the War Department's Directorate of Mechanization, which decided experiments and trials. Pile championed the experimental 16-tonners, and wished that Carden had "produced something startling in the way of medium tanks." Carden, however, still lacked experience and interest beyond tankettes.

> Carden became a great friend of mine and on many occasions he told me what an inspiration Liddell Hart had been to him. He used to say: "Whatever the General Staff may think, speed and armour as visualized by Liddell Hart must be the outstanding land weapon of the next war" (Pile 1965: 171).

During 1928, the British Army reclassified tankettes as "machine-gun carriers," and clarified their role as fire support. Also in 1928, Carden-Loyd's Mark VI carrier arrived – the most produced, used, exported, and copied platform in its class. Liddell Hart welcomed it as a tank. Martel was upset with the WD's and Liddell Hart's relegation of the Morris-Martel tankettes. He conceived extreme classes, from one-man "mechanical coffin" to land battleship, and refuted Liddell Hart's conflation of tanks with tankettes. In August, he returned Liddell Hart's commission to write on "Tanks" for *Encyclopaedia Britannica* (to LH, 9 August 1928, LHCMA LH 1/492 Part 1).

Carden-Loyd Carrier Mark VI in final form, in 1929, with amored covers over the crew positions.

Liddell Hart refused to refer to "machine-gun carriers." Reporting on the maneuvers of 1928, he refers interchangeably to "tanks" and "armoured machine guns." He rarely specifies weight classes, but uses "light tank," "tankette," "baby tank," and "midget tank" interchangeably. He expects even the 12-ton Vickers tanks to be replaced by tankettes (1929c: 99).

> A better course, certainly, might have been to proceed at once with the creation of a real all-armoured force, but in default of adequate light tanks there was a promise of benefit, especially moral, in trying how the infantry might be resuscitated by an infusion of Carden-Loyds (1932c: 200; 1935: 174).

Machine-gun carriers continued to be used in lieu of tanks, which added to the confusion. In 1929, all Carden-Loyd Mark VI carriers were consolidated under the two "experimental infantry brigades" (6th Brigade at Aldershot, 7th at Southern Command), for experiments in force structure. Liddell Hart misreported each brigade as "comprising one light-tank battalion and three new-pattern infantry battalions, the latter each having a mechanized machine-gun company" (1932c: 200; 1935: 174). In fact, these brigades never accepted tanks.

In 1929, the War Department tried Carden-Loyd's Light Tank Mark I (a turreted version of the machine-gun carrier). Liddell Hart got himself in a pickle. The light tank and carrier carry the same crewmen and armament and automotive line. In denigrating the tank, Liddell Hart unintentionally denigrated the tankette. This is clearest in his reassertion of Martel's "One-Man Tank." He complains that the latest doctrine (*Mechanised and Armoured Formations*, April 1929) specifies only medium and light tanks, not the tankette "originally intended" to accommodate just one man. He claimed that the Army's lack of confidence in the capacity of one man to both drive and fire at the same time is due to the stereotypical soldier's "manpower obsession" (1932c: 216; 1935: 190). He misreported that Martel had "proved" that one man could both drive the vehicle and fire its machine-gun at the same time. (In fact, Martel never fitted a machine-gun.) He explained away the War Department's insistence on at least two crewmen per carrier as accommodation for soldiers half as competent as Martel. He misrepresents Martel's "One-Man Tank" as more mobile than any tank across country, faster than any car on road, and stealthier than any tank. He imagines a tankette covering a mile across country in 3-4 minutes (15-20 mph), where a pedestrian would take 30 minutes (2 mph). He imagines it immune from small arms. He admits that a "large machine-gun" could destroy it, but claims that "numbers would be the best safeguard against the special anti-tank weapons." He imagines that no firearms could hit a tankette that is both moving and firing "a hail-storm of bullets most disturbing to his opponent's accuracy of aim" (1929c: 101-102; 1932c: 179-181). He does not admit that the tankette-gunner's aim would be disturbed by the tankette's movement.

Contradicting his faith in the "One-Man Tank," Liddell Hart offered the two-man Carden-Loyd machine-gun carriers as "baby tanks."

> This summer some 250 of these Carden-Loyds (fitted with Ford engines) were issued to the troops, part of them being used as light tanks and part as armoured machine-gun carriers for the infantry. Meantime an improved Carden-Loyd light tank has been designed – with thicker armour and more powerful motor, slightly larger, and considerably faster – and is under trial.
>
> As the invention of the first fast medium tanks portended the revival of cavalry's old decisive role, so the "baby" tank promises not only to amplify this role, but to replace infantry except in very wooded or mountainous country. It may be regarded as a revival of the old dragoons or mounted infantry, with the additional advantage of armour, so that it can not only move swiftly from point to point like its horsed forerunners, but can preserve and use this mobility on the battlefield.
>
> To realize its advantages let us compare it with the present infantryman. To close with his opponent he may often have to cross a space of a mile under machine-gun fire and rifle fire. Hampered by his equipment and the need of stopping to fire, he can rarely hope to traverse this space in less than half an hour, and often longer. And all the time his body is exposed to bullets, unless the ground is very broken or wooded. In contrast, the "light tankman" can be across and on top of his foe within five or six minutes. During this short exposure his body is protected by armour against bullets, except armour-piercing bullets fired by a special weapon [heavy machine-gun]. Moreover, he can fire as he moves, and although his "moving" fire may not be accurately aimed, it will create a "hail-storm" of bullets most disturbing to his opponent's accuracy of aim.
>
> Compared with the larger tank, the "baby's" advantage lies in its small-ness and invisibility. This advantage is multiplied by numbers, which is the old infantry principle – in new form – of dispersion to avoid enemy fire. These numbers are the best safeguard against the special anti-tank weapons which an enemy may possess, and are made possible by the relative cheapness of the [baby] tank (1929c: 101-102).

In the final maneuvers of 1929, the 6th Brigade was on the nominal invading side, against the 7th Brigade.

The result, certainly, has been to persuade the average infantryman of the advantage of going to battle in an armoured "pill-box" instead of on his flat feet! And the difficulty has been to induce him to use his Carden-Loyds as supporting weapons, and not to use them as storm-troops (1929c: 105).

Liddell Hart resented the use of the experimental infantry brigades to screen and to assault, when he wanted all tankettes transferred to a permanent tank brigade – to raid behind enemy lines, over days, without other arms. He once again misterms tankettes as light tanks.

[T]here was no question that the inclusion of light tanks greatly increased the offensive power of the infantry brigade. In practice, indeed, they formed the real assaulting troops, and the infantry battalions were little more than a supplement for "mopping up" and taking over captured ground. But one questioned at the time whether this benefit to the infantry brigade was not purchased at the expense of the whole – whether it was adequate compensation for the loss of strategic mobility and effect which in war would result from tying tanks so closely to infantry. The doubt was generally shared, and the subsequent removal of the light-tank battalions from the two Experimental Brigades[,] and their return to an independent tank formation, came as an answer to the question (1932c: 203; 1935: 177).

He resented particularly Carden-Loyd's tractor-trailer combination, designed for hauling the Oerlikon 20-mm fully-automatic anti-tank cannon and its crew to an emplacement. He misreports (perhaps wilfully) that the tractor-trailer competes with the machine-gun carrier in the same roles. Thence, he complains that it "costs nearly as much as, and is far less agile than, the light tank" (1932c: 256; 1935: 230).

For soldiers and civilians alike were provided with many good chuckles by the "three-piece" miniature road-train which cumbrously hauled the new anti-tank guns – with the gun pointing to the rear while in motion and so far less tactically efficient than its mobile quarry, the tank. Again it really did not require a prolonged and varied series of tests to ascertain that a cross-country machine of the Carden-Loyd type, little and low, was a better means of bringing the machine-gun into action than by the old horse-limber and manhandling. And better also than the unarmoured six-wheeler or any form of large armoured pantechnicon. Yet the simple deduction was to some extent obscured by the "brain wave" of attaching to each Carden-Loyd a four-seater trailer on tracks – admirably calculated to nullify their advantages. So long as the trailer is retained the extra load will inevitably reduce the mobility of the machine-gun carrier. Secondly, in contrast to the two-man crew of the armoured carrier, the four men in the trailer are exposed to fire. Further, as they decrease mobility, they also increase visibility – and vulnerability – for the carrier is not only slower in reaching a fire-position, but has less chance of reaching it unobserved, if it pulls a trailer behind (1932c: 201-202; 1935: 175-176).

Meanwhile, he repeats his claim from 1927 that tankettes (still misdescribed as light tanks) outmatch artillery.

> The anti-tank machine-gun is certainly a more dangerous obstacle than the field gun. It is easier to conceal; its fire is harder to spot and more easily switched in a new direction. There is, however, some compensation in the fact that its sting is less fatal. And the gun is hard to move – unless it is mounted in a tank. The best antidote certainly lies in the light tank. For this offers only a small target and it is far more agile than the anti-tank gun; its two-man crew enjoy the protection of armour, while the crew of the anti-tank gun are exposed (1932c: 250; 1935: 224).

He claimed that in 1929 "candid artillerymen [had] said frankly that they could not hope to hit such tiny machines. Candid infantrymen confessed that they felt as helpless as if attacked by a swarm of bees" (1932c: 219; 1935: 193). During the maneuvers in September 1930, he reported the Carden-Loyd machine-gun carrier as so small and stealthy as to creep up "within a few hundred yards" of entrenched infantry, to "catch them unawares from a close-up position or, alternatively, dismount and stalk them on foot" (1930c: 685; 1932c: 215; 1935: 189, 200). In 1931, he claimed that tankettes "not only merge with the background more easily [than horses], but attract the eye less in movement" 1932c: 226; 1935: 200). He admitted that tankettes struggle "in crossing ditches or crashing through hedges," but still claimed that they are sufficiently mobile to be "invulnerable." He characterized them as "immature" designs, with capacity for more mobility. He admitted he was proselytizing "to make officers picture the result of an attack by several hundreds – or thousands" (1932c: 219; 1935: 193). Somehow, he imagined that tankettes could see emplaced guns, but approach "unseen." Somehow, he imagined that guns "would have to shift their position – and thus disclose themselves," while "agile" tankettes dance around them. Somehow, he imagined that large-caliber armor-piercing bullets fired by heavy machine-guns could not penetrate the tankette's armor, while the tankette's light machine-gun would be "smothering them with bursts of fire from various directions" (1932c: 1935: 224).

He contradicts himself in the same book. In the context of the maneuvers of 1931, he admits that the carriers are inferior to turreted versions.

> The speed of the onsweep would have been still more impressive if armoured machine-gun carriers had not still been compelled to do duty as light tanks. Suited for working with infantry it was a strain on them not only to keep up but to keep ahead of this fast-moving tank force in its rapid bounds across steep spurs and rain-sodden ground (1932c: 255: 1935: 229).

In the context of the maneuvers of 1932, he admits that "the little Carden-Loyd machine-gun carriers…have long striven to fulfil a fast light-tank role beyond their powers" (1935: 267). Still, he champions Martel's one-man "mechanical coffin."

> Such an addition does not supersede the need for a proportion of "armoured infantry" – but a hope of the latter development is held out by the intended revival of experiments with the armoured machine-gun carrier, in which the gun is mounted on the vehicle and fires from it, although normally when halted.
>
> There are possibilities also in the idea embodied in a tiny box-like

machine, invented by Colonel Martel, who produced the first light tank. Its build is aptly indicated in its nickname of "mechanical coffin"; for it is only 7 feet long, 2 ½ feet wide (in the present one-man type), and stands only 20 inches above the ground – barely knee high. Propelled by a 4 h.p. motor, it will hold a light machine-gunner lying flat, and will carry him much faster (about 5·6 mph) than if he tried to crawl (1935: 264-265).

The General Staff wanted mediums for leading infantry in assaults. However, British industry was not developing mediums, except when the War Department allocated its own design and production authorities as partners. Britain's tank industry preferred to develop small, light vehicles, given the larger export market. Vickers (which acquired Carden-Loyd in 1928) exported more tankettes than tanks. Vickers held a near monopoly in British armaments, but regarded ground vehicles as a minor concern next to warships and aircraft. From 1929 until 1939, the only tanks acquired by the British Army in more than experimental numbers were Vickers Light tanks, each weighing between 3 and 5 long tons. They were distinguished from the Carden-Loyd carrier, from which they evolved, by only their turret – not their armament or crew count, until the three-man Mark V of 1934.

Liddell Hart contributed to the distortion by peddling myths that carriers are tanks, tanks can be crewed by just one man, and that a ban on armored vehicles over 5 long tons (5.6 short tons) would disable offenses. He lobbied for such a ban, both to the officials preparing for the world disarmament conference, and as a journalist. His lobbying was acute from 1930 (when the conference was agreed) and 1932 (when the conference convened). He repeated his proposal during World War II and after (1932b: 73-76; 1940: 166; 1965: I, 183-184, 186-190, 206-207; Noel-Baker 1936: 195, 239-240, 268-269; Temperley 1938: 195; Noel Baker 1979: 61).

Independent of a ban on AFVs over 5 tons, he imagined that the proliferation of machine-guns and "the diminution of heavier weapons – artillery and tanks" mean that "none of the armies possess the offensive power" they had possessed during the Great War (1932c: 165; 1935: 151).

> Any invasion, save in mountainous country, will depend for success on the quantity of heavy guns and tanks. These, indeed, are the only forms of force which make an advance possible under modern conditions against an up-to-date opponent (1932c: 167; 1935: 153).

Quantity is not his only hope for offensive success. He argues that bombers and light AFVs are fast and evasive enough to attack into enemy territory. In turn, bombers are among the weapons (the others are machine-guns, landmines, and fortifications) that render useless all but the lightest AFVs, he argues. Despite welcoming light tanks, he kept cycling back to tankettes. Early in 1931, he lectured to Southern Command on "The Future of Infantry." He compares medium and heavy tanks to a stealthier, more efficient, "cheap baby tank," "miniature tank," "machine-gun carrier," and "armoured carrier." One of his false claims is that a tankette reduces six machine-gun crewmen to two, as if nobody is sustaining the machine-gun or the vehicle (1932c: 131, 221; 1935: 117, 195).

> A more promising line of tank development, and, in my opinion, the trend of the future, lies in the direction of the miniature tank, built mainly from commercial motor parts, so that cheapness in peace and quantity

> production in case of war can be ensured. This line was initiated in England with the experimental "one-man tanks" of 1925, invented by Martel and Carden. Since then much progress has been made, and although they now have a crew of two they are still so small and low – lower than a man's height – as to be almost invisible targets, whilst their improved performance is obtained at a cost, which, according to type, varies between that of a Buick and a Rolls-Royce touring car. In mass production it would, of course, be reduced...
>
> These inconspicuous vehicles, of high speed and remarkable track endurance, have covered long road journeys as quickly and easily as an ordinary motor car, and to travel in them across rolling downland is more comfortable than in a motor-car, even a six-wheeled car. At present only some 60 in all have been provided, and only one light-tank battalion [actually, a mechanized infantry battalion] has been tentatively formed. But it is worth emphasis that a handy fighting unit of 50 such machines would have greater fire-power than an infantry battalion of 1,000 men, cost less to maintain, and would multiply its actual fire-power by the rapidity with which it could be switched from point to point (1932c: 129, 179; 1935: 115).

Here he proposes to cut 90 percent of men in each infantry battalion, far beyond his legacy proposal to cut 50 percent of men and one-third of infantry battalions (1927b: 12; 1932c: 245; 1935: 194, 219). This becomes another hope for disarmament.

> The army which first had the moral courage to scrap most of its old-style units and replace them by a small number of mobile armoured units would at once enjoy an immense advantage over all others. The armies of the world would be thrown into the melting pot, and from this might emerge not only a general new pattern but a real opportunity for an agreement upon the reduction of land armaments. Soldiers perhaps suspect this, or feel it subconsciously, and hence are the more dubious of change...The best chance of change lies with the development of the cheap baby tank such as the Carden (1932c: 130; 1935: 116).

As ever, his argument assumes that only tankettes can survive machine-guns.

> Once a number of these armoured carriers are provided for the machine-guns of every infantry battalion, soldiers may begin to ask themselves whether 800 slow-moving and non-bullet-proof riflemen are necessary as well. They may feel that more machines and fewer men would give greater chances of success – besides saving men's pay in peace and widows' pensions in war. The machine-gun has proved itself the dominating weapon on modern battlefields, and there is no logical reason why they should be limited to a mere 16 per battalion now that, through armour and the petrol motor, they can take a direct part in the attack and ensure themselves an adequate supply of ammunition (1932c: 131; 1935: 117).

His faith in aircraft was popular, but his faith in tankettes was subject to parody. For instance, Evelyn Waugh wrote a novel ("Black Mischief") from September 1931 to May 1932, in which an African Emperor, educated in England and obsessed with

European "modernization," tells his English adviser: "Soon we have no more soldiers. Tanks and aeroplanes. That is modern. I have seen it." The Emperor acquires only one "tank" – a two-man tankette that becomes so hot as to be inoperable after 5 miles, and is repurposed as a punishment chamber.

Waugh's fictional African Emperor was based on the Emperor of Abyssinia (Haile Selassie), where the Italians deployed copies of the Carden-Loyd Carrier Mark VI, which they classified as "fast tanks" (abbreviated as "CV" in Italian). Only the Soviet Union acquired more tankettes in the independent role pushed by Martel and Liddell Hart. The Italian Army, unlike the Red Army, deleted its legacy light and medium tanks, except for home defence (until resurrecting the requirements in 1939). Liddell Hart praised this choice.

> A few years ago it was ill[-]furnished with heavy guns and tanks, but has begun to repair its deficiencies...That the Italians are perceptive of the value of speed is shown by the fact that they have recently acquired a considerable number of British Carden-Loyds – the miniature tank or armoured machine-gun carrier (1932c: 171, 177; 1935: 157).

The wars in Abyssinia (1935-1936) and Spain (1936-1939) disproved the utility of Italian tankettes. Liddell Hart paid little attention. By contrast, Fuller embedded with the Italian side in both wars. He again declared tankettes as useless. He submitted his observations and conclusions through confidential reports to the War Office, journalistic reports, and a book that he completed in late February 1937:

> [O]n account of cheapness, the existing light tank [tankette] was produced, a small run-about machine which proved of little use both in the Italo-Abyssinian and the Spanish Civil Wars. On account of this a revulsion in the favour of infantry has taken place, which, in my opinion, is in no way justified, not only because the machines used were of faulty design, but also because they were employed in the wrong way...

Panzer IA (right) and Panzer IB (left) tanks are parked in La Granadella, during the Nationalist advance on Barcelona, in January 1939. (The Panzer 1B has a larger engine, an extended rear, and a raised idler.) The Associated Press office in London described them as "light tanks, part of the up-to-date mechanised equipment which has helped the Franco armies to victory in the Catalonian offensive." Most Western journalists, most influentially Basil Liddell Hart, reported tanks as failures, without visiting.

A Bren Gun Carrier, as depicted in the War Office's "Photographs of Modern Equipments," officially issued on 8th November 1939.

Another criticism which is equally foolish is that as anti-tank weapons evolve the tank will ultimately become useless. But why? Here arises the old problem of gun versus armour. What is armour for? Not to keep out all projectiles at all ranges – this has seldom been possible; but instead, to keep out the bulk of the enemy's projectiles at all ranges, so that his offensive power may be restricted to certain kinds of projectiles only (Fuller 1937: 137, 139).

Fuller's criticism of Italian tankettes was confirmed, just after he submitted this text, by the Italian-Spanish offensive at Guadalajara in March 1937. In April, Fuller reported privately that "account should be taken of the fact that the small German [Panzer I] and Italian tanks, which have been employed in Spain, were already recognized as too small." By contrast, in December Liddell Hart reported this offensive as evidence for the defensive advantages of aircraft, and hoped that the Italians had lost confidence in "tanks" (1939b: 54, 101, 105; 1944: 35; Wright 2000: 215).

In September 1936, Martel visited the Soviet maneuvers, which featured the most-produced tankette anywhere. The T27 is a larger, fully-enclosed derivative of a Carden-Loyd Carrier Mark VI that had been imported in 1930. The T27 was issued from 1931, for reconnaissance, screening, and counter-insurgency. Both the Soviets and Martel classified the type as "tankette." Martel honestly reported that the Soviets "do not put much faith in these machines, and do not seem to have worked out the tactical conception for their employment." Martel leaked his report to Liddell Hart, but Liddell Hart chose to report only the Soviet light and light-medium tanks (Martel to LH, 21 October 1936, LH 1/492 Part 2).

In 1932, Liddell Hart had learned of a prospective three-man Bren Gun Carrier. He resented its size and role (fire-support), but welcomed it as partial fulfilment of his prior requirement for tankettes. In 1934, he learned of prospective variants – one to carry the 3-inch mortar, another the Vickers medium machine-gun, which he rejected as unnecessary. He learned of them during an invited visit to the General Staff department for force structure (SD2), a day before a public briefing. Colonel

Gordon Macready made clear that the Carriers are fire-support vehicles, not tanks.

> The object of these armoured carriers is to enable machine-guns to advance rapidly over fire-swept zones and to come into action, if necessary, from the vehicle though not on the move, as the latter would practically necessitate the provision of a tank. The machine-gun will, of course, be capable of being taken out of the vehicle and fired from the ground when required. These armoured carriers, if found to be successful, would be incorporated in the companies of the machine-gun battalion (Macready 1935: 12).

Liddell Hart wanted carriers to replace all the light tanks in each division's mechanized cavalry battalion, and most of the infantry in each infantry battalion. He claimed that each unit could be reduced to one company of Bren Gun Carriers. The WD preferred Macready's plan. Bren Gun Carriers were issued to machine-gun battalions from 1935. Liddell Hart hoped to influence a change when he became adviser to a new, flamboyant War Secretary (Leslie Hore Belisha) in May 1937. In September, Belisha, Liddell Hart, and Macready visited the final British and French maneuvers of the year. Macready was most impressed with French use of two-man carriers, with trailers, as supply vehicles. He instigated requirements for unarmed carriers and tractors, later fulfilled by variants of the Bren Gun Carrier and new unarmored competitors. Liddell Hart resented these requirements as distractions, and never reported them (1965: II, 30; Macready 1965: 104).

On 10 March 1938, the Army Estimates (the annual presentation to Parliament by the War Department for the upcoming fiscal year) included the provision of one platoon of carriers to each infantry battalion. A year later, when this provision was approaching fulfilment, Liddell Hart repeated his preference to delete machine-gun battalions, and mortar and medium machine-gun carriers, in order to release Bren Gun Carriers to the infantry, at every echelon. He wrote that Bren Gun Carriers "meant that the infantry would have small armoured fighting vehicles of their own, thus bringing to fruition an idea I had mooted as far back as 1919." In fact, back then he had required an unarmed armored carrier for each platoon's supplies and equipment, i.e., something closer to Macready's requirement for unarmed carriers and tractors (1919b: 666-667; 1939b: 313-314).

In June 1939, Liddell Hart claimed credit for 62 "reforms" in the two years he had been advising Belisha. His "reforms" mention no vehicles except Bren Gun Carriers, which he describes as "armoured carriers, mounting light machine-guns." Two months later, the Second World War started. During the war, he described the type as an "armoured carrier, a miniature tank" (1939b: 327; 1941: 28n).

Liddell Hart's requirements were more foresightful in 1919 than 1941. In the Second World War, the dominant role for the Bren Gun Carrier and its variants was as an unarmed carrier of equipment and supplies. By then, the dominant variant was the four-man Universal Carrier, although all variants were described, out of habit, as Bren Gun Carriers.

After 1919, Liddell Hart had taken his requirement for armored carriers in the wrong direction – away from a platoon's equipment and supplies to one machine-gun and two crewmen. During the Second World War, the Army belatedly realized a requirement for an armored carrier to carry a platoon's men and equipment. This was fulfilled with surplus tanks and self-propelled guns – after removal of their main armament. This fulfilment repeated a solution adopted during the First World War. Liddell Hart had not foreseen its revival.

Tankettes and machine-gun carriers disappeared by the end of the Second World War, except for the four-man Universal Carrier, in British and Commonwealth use, and legacy tankettes in Italian service. After the war, Liddell Hart pretended that his advocacy for tankettes had been for proper tanks and platoon carriers. For instance, he cited an article from the 1920s (on tankettes) to suggest, in one letter, and in one chapter of a book, that he had advocated tanks, of the types that matured during the Second World War. However, in another letter (to the same person), and in another chapter (of the same book), he claimed that he had advocated for tankettes to become armored personnel carriers, of the types that matured during the Second World War (to Ogorkiewicz, 16 August 1949 and 17 August 1961, RACTM E2015.2015.58 and .68; 1965: I, 78, 124-125, 178).

Liddell Hart's pre-war use of the word "tank" to refer to tankettes and carriers helped his post-war reinvention. The Second World War persuaded everybody that tankettes, carriers, and tanks are technologically and doctrinally different after all, but he never gave up his hopes for light tanks, as explained in the next chapter.

British soldiers train with a Kangaroo (class name for personnel carrier), converted from a US-supplied M7 Priest self-propelled 105-mm gun, and a US-supplied M29 Weasel carrier (unarmored), in Italy in 1945. The Weasel is amphibious by design. This Priest was adapted for deep wading with sealants and extensions to the air intake and exhaust.

CHAPTER 6

Light Tanks

The first Vickers Light series (since 1923) was reclassified as Medium in 1927, at around 12 long tons (13.4 short). A separate evolutionary line of Vickers Light Tanks was ordered in 1928. Carden lengthened and raised the two-man tankette platform, and added a one-man turret, to produce the Light Tank Mark I, at 3.25 long tons (3.6 short). This was tried from 1929.

Liddell Hart did not admit the advantage of a turret. Confusingly, he continued to conflate light tanks with "the tankettes which became infantry machine-gun carriers" (1935: 281). Yet he also started to relegate tankettes behind light tanks. His justification is speed. The Light Tank nominally offered an extra 5 mph in speed. However, it pitched more, so crews were unwilling to go full speed. Its greater advantages, for mobility, were abilities to cross taller steps, cross wider gaps, and pivot easier. He never mentioned these disadvantages and advantages. He reports that light tanks could maneuver "50 percent" faster than tankettes, without admitting any reasons other than maximum speed (1935: 273).* He imagines that light tanks and tankettes are fast enough to evade ground and air weapons. In fact, light tanks were rated for only 30 mph, on road, in a straight line. He resurrects his promise that increasing numbers of bombers and light tanks would strengthen the offensive, while increasing numbers of machine-guns would strengthen the defensive (1925: 42, 82-83; 1932c: 140-146; 1939b: 321). Thence, he forecasts victory to the side preponderant in bombers and light tanks (1925: 9, 55; 1932c: 134, 181, 217-219; 1935: 120; 1939b: 157-161).

By 1930, he regards machine-guns, vehicles, and numbers as most useful to the defensive. He acknowledges that "new gas and tank weapons [enable a] break through the opposing line," but concludes that "machine-guns are more numerous than ever in proportion to numbers of men, while the use of gas is banned and the use of tanks is on a puny experimental scale" (1932c: 118; 1935: 104). He imagines that light tanks and carriers are immune to normal bullets, thanks to armor, small size, mobility, and numbers, but that machine-guns are sufficient to defeat other tanks. Here he specifies medium machine-guns, which, as currently defined by the British Army, fire the same 0.303-inch caliber rounds as light machine-guns, but benefit from water-cooling (1932c: 178). He champions medium machine-guns for both pedestrians and tanks, on the grounds of portability. Bizarrely, he reserves medium machine-guns for carriers and light tanks, because he imagines that heavy machine-guns (0.5-inch or 12.7-mm) would make vehicles too large, heavy, and slow. He concludes that heavy machine-guns should be reserved as static defensive weapons. Even more bizarrely, he imagines that static machine-guns would stop tanks but not tankettes. He admits that "large machine-guns" could perforate the

---

* He miscalculated: in performance of a tactical exercise, the light tanks were actually 40 percent faster, according to the numbers on the same page and in unit diaries.

A Light Tank Mark I, delivered in 1929, a Medium Mark II, and A6E2 (the second of the 16-tonners, delivered in 1928)

armor on "light tanks," but imagines that small size, speed, and numbers would "safeguard" them (1932c: 181). He asserts the "light tank's…invulnerability through smallness of target" (1932c: 217; 1935: 191). He touts the new Vickers amphibious tank (a two-man turreted tank with armor up to 11 mm thick) as immune against armor-piercing bullets at 150 yards. In fact, 0.5-inch steel-cored bullets reliably penetrate 1 inch (25.4 mm) at 100 yards, far beyond the thickness of any tank in British service (1932c: 182; DCIGS, "57/Tanks/222 - Tank and Anti-Tank Design," 29 August 1921, RACTM E1963.46.10).

Contradictorily, he concedes that "heavy tanks" are more survivable and lethal and thus more capable of offensives (and counter-offensives). However, he wants to ban offensive weapons. He classifies all armored vehicles over 5 long tons as "heavy tanks." He asserts that only light tanks and carriers can succeed offensively. This offensive utility is nuanced, because he prefers raids over assaults. His desire to avoid the costs of assaults is justifiable, but his optimism about raids is not. He imagines that lighter tanks, given higher speed, smaller size, and lower logistical burden, could evade enemy defensive and counter-offensive forces, strike artillery, industry, and infrastructure in the enemy's rear, and escape days later.

In 1931, he claimed that a single Mark I (two men and a machine-gun) offers "far more effective striking power than an infantry section" (about nine men, eight rifles, and a machine-gun), for "less than half" the operating cost. From these unsourced mathematics, he promises savings to pay for light tanks (1932c: 256; 1935: 230).

> In quantity of such machines lies one means to discount the inevitable toll taken by anti-tank guns. The other means lies in the reborn Mongol tactics which were so well brought out in the exercises [of August 1931] (1932c: 256; 1935: 230).

In addition to raiding, he requires light tanks for counter-insurgency.

> The British have been more concerned with the problem of operations on the frontiers of empire – the recurrent type of colonial war or insurrection. Here, the opponents would lack a powerful or numerous artillery; speed, reliability[,] and agility would be the important needs, so long as the tanks were proof against bullets. Another factor was the rise of a distinctively British school of thought who perceived a wider horizon of mechanical warfare. We argued that the tanks were the heirs of the now moribund cavalry; that tanks could be used, like the cavalry of old, for

decisive manoeuvres against the enemy's rear, cutting off his supplies and menacing his line of retreat, so that first paralysis and then panic might set in. Gradually these ideas permeated the Army, although new equipment has been slower than new thought (1932c: 174-175).

In effect, he touts the least lethal and least survivable armored vehicles as the best platforms for offensives, restricts offensive platforms to light or medium machine-guns, imagines that larger guns contribute to only the defense, dismisses heavier tanks as too costly, burdensome, and targetable, downgrades other arms, and opposes combined arms.

In 1931, the British Army tried the Vickers Light Tank Mark II. Its main advantage over the Mark I is a larger turret, on a squarer plan, to accommodate a radio in its rear. Yet Liddell Hart reported a revolutionary step in mobility.

> Only a bare dozen of the modern Mark II light tanks were yet available, and they were used mainly as "mounts" for commanders and liaison officers. With their squat toad-like chassis surmounted by a high, narrow turret they are excellently designed for stealing up behind a bush or crest, and "peeping" their turret machine guns over it. To watch them sweep forward is to perceive the menace that their speed, agility, and unobtrusiveness combined threaten to infantry and artillery. They are, in truth, an ominously looming cloud on the horizon of all old-style forces.

> But for that menace to be fulfilled those new and comparatively cheap machine-guns must be provided in sufficient quantity to form a tactical cloud. In driblets they may be merely useful, whereas in a deluge they would be decisive (1932c: 255; 1935: 229; 1944: 269).

The official historian of the Great War (a long-time collaborator) wrote with a caution. "Any tank which shows its nose in the open will in my opinion be knocked out at once...The wars you and Fuller imagine are past" (Brigadier-General Sir James Edmonds to Liddell Hart, 5 July 1932, LHCMA LH 1/259).

The maneuvers of 1932 included 50 Mark IIs, enough to complete the light tank battalion. Liddell Hart reported the type as sufficient for all tank requirements, in replacement of the mediums in the other battalions. He suggests that one light tank should be acquired for every two infantrymen (the historical rate of cavalrymen to infantrymen). This becomes his unadmitted justification for his estimate that "the annual cost of such a machine should, in mass production, approximate to that of a couple of infantrymen." By saving infantry, he promises one tank battalion per two infantry battalions. In 1934, he assessed the new 1st Tank Brigade, with just 600 men, as more lethal, survivable, and mobile than an infantry division at "war establishment," with 20,000 men (1933: 110; 1935: 267, 271, 277).

Also in 1934, he notes the fielding of "three-man light tanks" (nine incomplete Mark Vs), without praise or appraisal, likely because the larger turret, extra crewman (a gunner), and larger caliber (0.50-inch) machine-gun add weight, which reduces speed (1935: 281). He reiterates that fast tanks can evade air attack, ground defences, and natural obstacles, and raid industry and infrastructure in the enemy's rear, independently of other arms. They are "the ideal agents of infiltration" (1935: 267, 273; 1965: I, 224). Here he specifies light tanks as turreted, but still wants them armed the same as tankettes, lest they get bigger and heavier (1935: 55-56).

Vickers Light Mark VI and Medium Mark II tanks on Salisbury Plain in August 1938, as depicted in *The Times* **newspaper, above one of Liddell Hart's reports.**

He does not want tanks to fight tanks, which he regards as distractions from non-combatant targets in the enemy's rear. In the same year, Erich Ludendorff (Germany's effective supreme commander, from 1916 to 1918) released a book, stating: "The final decision on land will lie in the fight of man against man, tank against man, or tank against tank." Liddell Hart complained: "how a tank can destroy a tank, any more than a warship can destroy a warship, except by fire, Ludendorff does not explain" (1936b: 689). Indeed, Liddell Hart's preferred tanks could not destroy each other, so long as he assumed their immunity to the same machine-guns he specified as armament.

Effective in 1934, Percy Hobart took command of the Tank Brigade (and the Inspectorate of the Royal Tank Corps), consulted Liddell Hart on all-tank raids, and adopted Liddell Hart's assumptions. For instance, he promised that metallurgical developments would improve engines and armor, more than anti-tank capabilities (IRTC to DSD, 22 March 1935, LHCMA Lindsay).

Liddell Hart admitted the growth in the quantity and quality of anti-tank guns, but promised more and faster light tanks. From late October 1936, he published in *The Times* a series of arguments to reduce garrisons overseas to pedestrians, home forces to anti-aircraft divisions, and the expeditionary force ("Field Force") to a port garrison, with "swarms" of fast tanks to raid in the enemy's rear. His article of 2 November develops this quantitative argument.

> [T]he post-war development of anti-tank weapons is a serious and increasing threat to the tank, especially when coupled with the new technique of obstruction. How serious, it is not easy to gauge. We can at least be clear that the chances of the tank increase with their quantity – and decrease proportionately when they are few. At present we seem to contemplate no more than our one existing tank brigade, re-equipped with modern machines – which would form part of a mobile division otherwise possessing small power of attack – and four battalions of infantry[-support] tanks still to be built. With so few tanks the chances of successful attack might well be zero. Against the multiplying anti-tank weapons of today it is certain that hope lies only in swarms – to swamp the defence (1937: 140-141; 1941: 117).

Liddell Hart's "hope" for "swarms" is contradicted by his hope for defence-dominance. This is clearer in a version of the above published in December.

> Armour, in the form of the tank, proved a better means in the last war of helping the attack forward; but armour used in a direct assault against organized defence would now seem to have lost much of its value through the great and widespread development of armour-piercing weapons — there are now highly efficient anti-tank machine guns, and even rifles, as well as guns (1936b: 692-693).

By contrast, Fuller (1937: 129-131, 137, 140-141, 160, 217) described the tank as "the master land weapon" because it protects and attacks all land weapons.

Liddell Hart never scaled the "swarm" necessary to defeat defence-dominance. At times, he implies thousands of light tanks. The article published on 30 October states that "the nominal 200 tanks of our solitary Tank Brigade are a puny total compared with the thousands of tanks in the chief Continental armies." At this time, the British Army held 280 light and 166 medium tanks. Its intelligence staff estimated that Germany possessed 1,600 light tanks and 300-400 medium tanks, and that France possessed 500-600 light tanks and 130 medium tanks. Even if all French tanks would combine with all British tanks, Liddell Hart needs thousands of light tanks to "swarm" 2,000 German tanks. He would need more thousands to swarm German anti-tank guns and to survive German aircraft (Brigadier O.E. Chapman, "Design and Production of British Tanks," Part 1, "1936-June 1940 (Preliminary Draft)," circa January 1944, RACTM 355.6 Tank Supply, Box 2).

Wary of criticisms of his quantitative argument, he returned to the fantasy that technological change favors light tanks. For instance, he misreported the Mark VIb Light, delivered in June 1938 with minor changes to the Mark VIa's powerplant, as dramatically more survivable.

> The production of the latest type light tanks has been going well. It is reported that well before the end of 1938 the rate at which these were coming through had risen to about three a day; and that they can already be counted in their hundreds. Moreover, they are likely to alter current ideas as to the comparative vulnerability of light tanks, being much better protected, without serious increase of weight, than any of the home or foreign machines of this kind which have been seen hitherto. That also applies to the new cruiser tanks. Whereas the anti-tank side has been gaining for several years past, in the unceasing competition between armour and armour-piercing weapons, an important step forward has now been made in our tank design towards nullifying the effect of a large proportion of the anti-tank weapons now existing (1939b: 322).

In September 1938, during the crisis over Germany's demands for its Sudetenland in Czechoslovakia, he undermined his argument for "swarms" of light tanks, by prioritizing bombers for the Royal Air Force, heavy anti-aircraft guns for home forces, and lighter small arms, anti-aircraft guns, and indirect-fire artillery for any expeditionary force. Increasingly, he argued that the Field Force is unnecessary, given defense-dominance on the ground and offense-dominance in the air. His last peacetime book (published June 1939) ridicules German, Italian, and Soviet confidence in the offensive potential of tanks (1939b: 92-94). He argues that automobiles, particularly armored vehicles, are useful for a defensive "counter-stroke," but somehow not for an offensive strike, while aircraft are best for both counter-strokes and offensives (1939b: 121).

After the Second World War, both Liddell Hart and Martel pretended that their advocacy for tankettes should be credited for the light tanks normalized during the war – despite more crewmen, thicker armour, and heavier artillery than most of the medium tanks that had started the war (1965: I, 78, 178; Martel 1945: 18; Martel 1949: 66, 73). The war required much heavier tanks in each class. Light tanks grew from around 5 tons to nearly 20 tons, medium tanks from less than 15 tons to more than 30, and heavy tanks from 25 tons to more than 50, while super-heavy tanks remained around 75 tons. By 1949, Liddell Hart himself admitted that the "weight of the main types of tank in use has approximately trebled in the last ten years – as a result of continuous efforts to mount a bigger gun and thicker armour." However, he opposed these trends (1950: 213; 1960: 193).

By 1943, Martel required heavy tanks to compete with the German Tiger and Panther, but he and Liddell Hart subsequently fell out. In November 1945, General Wilhelm von Thoma, who had commanded German light tanks from Spain (1936) to North Africa (1942), told Liddell Hart they were "sardine-tins" that "he did not count" in the total deployed against France. When given a binary choice, Thoma conceded that he would choose speed over armor, but added that he would allow for only one-third of tanks in the ideal regiment to sacrifice armor. General Hasso von Manteuffel similarly conceded that speed "is the most important lesson of the war in regard to tank design," but his exemplar is the Panther, which the Western Allies categorized as heavy. The Panther (45 metric tons) and Tiger (56 metric tons) could reach almost 30 mph, proving that tanks could combine more speed, armor, and armament than Liddell Hart and Hobart ever expected. Despite this evidence, Liddell Hart continued to claim that the Germans were influenced most by British light tanks, whose cheapness outweighed their "inherent limitations" (notes on talk with Thoma, 1 November 1945, LHCMA LH 9/24/144; 1948: 125, 99; to Ogorkiewicz, 16 August 1949, RACTM E2015.2015.58; 1950: 25; 1959: 237).

Medium A or Whippet tanks were first used in March 1918. This one is viewed from its left front. The tower was designed with a machine-gun mounting in four sides, and a driver's position at its right front.

CHAPTER 7

Medium Tanks

Vickers had delivered Light Mark I tanks first in 1923, Light Mark II Tanks in 1925, before they were reclassified as mediums in 1927. Each is taller and better armed than the mediums of the Great War, but lighter. The latest variants weighed 12 tons, compared to 14 tons of the first wartime mediums. Each accommodated five men, six machine-guns, and a 47-mm 3-pounder gun. However, armor was no thicker than 8 mm, compared to 14 mm on prior medium and later light tanks.

Once the British Army reclassified its first lights as mediums, Liddell Hart dismissed them as "an interim and an expensive weapon." He pushed tankettes and light tanks (most of them weighing one-quarter as much) as sufficient for all "tank" requirements – from the cavalry's scouting, screening and pursuit roles to the Tank Corps' assault role. Contradictorily, he required "a larger tank, strongly armoured and with a heavier armament" (1927a: 80).

His requirement for "a larger tank" would be short-lived. From 1930, he classed all armored vehicles over 5 long tons as "heavy tanks," in hope of an international ban. Nevertheless, the 12-ton Mediums grew on him. After the maneuvers of 1931, he praised them as an under-appreciated light or "fast type." At that moment, he required only tankettes and light tanks for screening, and only 12-ton Mediums for assaulting. His justifications are speed and stealth, even though the Mediums are half as quick and 1.5 times taller than current light tanks. His current misperception seems to be anchored in a particularly subjective impression. On a misty morning in August 1931, he had found them "often indistinguishable from bushes" (1932c: 226, 255; 1935: 200, 229). One explanation is his short-sightedness. Another explanation is his preference for observing from a luxury car.

> Even though one knew the exact, and small, area in which they were working, and was following them in a car, it was difficult to locate them. Time after time companies of tanks were swallowed up on some fold of the ground, to emerge suddenly close to their prey. While the noise of their tracks gave some warning of their stealthy approach, it was a deceptive noise to locate, and the presence of so large a number of tanks confused the listener (1932c: 257; 1935: 231).

> To follow such a battle one really needs a cross-country vehicle faster than the tanks themselves; but even then one would often be baffled because of the ground-craft developed by some of the tank leaders (1935: 274).

Contradictorily, he concludes from the same maneuvers that the "Medium" is "massive" enough to overrun field guns (1932c: 250; 1935: 224). In a contradiction of a contradiction, he "doubts whether such shock action" by "medium tanks" "could increase the chaos that would be caused by a driving storm of bullets at close

Medium IIIE2 is used as the Tank Brigade's command tank in Summer 1934, by Brigadier Percy Hobart, next to General "Jock" Burnett-Stuart of Southern Command.

range" from tankettes (1932c: 252; 1935: 228).

From 1926, Vickers, the Directorate of Mechanization, and the Royal Ordnance Factories cooperated in a heavier medium tank. Various designs were delivered, of which the only products taken into service (in 1934) and mentioned by Liddell Hart are the three Medium Mark III tanks. Each Mark III weighed nearly 19 long tons, but they were marketed as "sixteen-tonners," the same as their ancestors (A6E1 and A6E2 in 1928, A6E3 in 1934). Liddell Hart scoffed at the offensive capacity of such "heavy" and thence slow tanks, even though they reached close to 30 mph (5mph shy of the latest light tanks). Yet his memoirs pretend that he supported the type (it "outclassed anything else in the world at the time of its appearance"), and that the British government turned to lighter tanks on cost alone (1935: 55-56; 1965, I: 278).

His contempt for the War Office probably explains his failure to mention the A7 projects, designed by the tracked vehicle section (DDM) of the Superintendent of Design, and built by the Carriage Factory, both at Woolwich Arsenal. A7E1 and A7E2 were delivered in 1933, with different suspensions. Their architecture, automotive line, and fighting arrangements were carried over to the A7E3. Hobart's and Liddell Hart's resistance to three-man turrets was one of the factors in A7E3's slow development, although outsourcing was another factor (AEC, the supplier of the power plant, was most problematic). A7E3 was not running until 17 October 1936, too late to be readied for a demonstration to politicians on 2 November (Ross diary, IWM; Ross 1976: 95-100; Birch, interview with MGO, 30 October 1936, RACTM E2011.1654). A7E3 was the best medium tank on offer, as its heavier derivative (Matilda II) would prove in 1940. A7E3 weighed slightly less than the Medium III. Yet Liddell Hart misreported British mediums of the 1930s as heavier and less reliable than cruiser tanks.

> During the next four years [1933-1936] little was achieved in tank design, development, or production – the inertia and shortsightedness of the

The Superintendent of Design's A7E1 in 1929.

Mechanization Board at Woolwich Arsenal contributed largely to this state of stagnation. A variety of experimental models were designed and tried, in a desultory way, and all proved unsatisfactory. More time was wasted in attempting to correct their mechanical faults, and by the time the worst of these troubles were remedied, the models were manifestly out of date and tactically inadequate (1965: I, 389).

Liddell Hart wanted to replace current medium tanks with light tanks, each accommodating only two men and a machine-gun.

> The cry for "bigger and better" machines has already raised the estimated cost of the light tank from £500 [Martel's one-man tankette] to £2,000, and, if the desire for thicker armour and higher power is not limited, it will end in another large tank – and so forfeit the supreme asset of invulnerability [smallness] of target (1932c: 217; 1935: 190).

During the maneuvers of 1932, he reported that the Medium Mark II tanks "are too old in years and too thin in armour plate for employment against a properly equipped modern army, although they might be formidable against tribesmen – so far as such aged machines could stand the mechanical strain." In 1933, he described them as "obsolete." In 1934, he described them as "death-traps on active service." These are fair assessments. Yet he opposed replacements of medium weight. He warned that tanks with armaments larger than a medium machine-gun would be too conspicuous and slow. In "the past year…armies are beginning to develop…the speed of their tanks" (1933: 110; 1935: 69, 258, 267).

Speed is an amateur's assumption of tank mobility. What about agility, step-climbing, trench-spanning, slope-climbing, wading, and soil flotation? Liddell Hart never specified these capabilities. The 1st Tank Brigade assembled in April 1934 with more tankettes than any other class of AFV. Brigadier Percy Hobart realized:

> The necessity for medium tanks was apparent throughout…The limitations of the two-man tank vis-à-vis the three-man tanks were again very apparent ("Report on Royal Tank Corps Staff Exercise at Cambridge 8-12 May 1934," LHCMA LH 15/11/6).

This helps to explain Liddell Hart's admission that the maneuvers of the year had "unintentionally" revealed that light tanks cannot cross "a wide ditch and steep bank" that medium tanks cross easily. Yet he still opposed heavier armament or armor (1935: 289). He did not adjust his opposition given what he heard from Macready inside SD2 and RUSI on 13 and 14 November respectively.

> For the last few years we have been experimenting with various types of anti-tank gun firing a solid bullet. But whilst these experiments have been going on the armour of tanks in foreign armies had tended to increase yearly. Moreover, it is, I think, becoming clearer every year that, while it is possible to obtain an anti-tank weapon firing a solid bullet which will penetrate any armour likely to be encountered at moderate ranges, such a weapon will not necessarily stop a tank. Also, if a really high performance is to be obtained, the weapon inevitably becomes too heavy to be handled by one man (Macready 1935: 12).

The maneuvers of 1935 proved Macready right and Liddell Hart wrong. One tank officer publicly rebutted Liddell Hart in all but name.

> The medium tank is at present too slow, very thinly armoured, very costly and as a result of its special machinery takes a long time to produce. Many officers advocate that we should abolish it and have light tanks only in the Tank Brigade. Although the proportion of light to medium tanks may be altered, the medium tank must always remain in considerable numbers. In the end, the answer to the tank is another tank. Therefore a high proportion of our tanks must carry guns, which will pierce the armour of any practical tank – say 1-inch [25.4 mm] – at 500 yards range at a 45-degree angle of impact. That is something of the size of the 3-pdr. Some mediums must carry 3-in. mortars, firing smoke or HE. The light tank is easily held up by small obstacles; the medium tank can cross these or flatten them out and form a "bridgehead," while the light tanks get across. The medium tank can crush, literally, enemy defences, knock down small houses and walls and fight the medium tanks of the enemy. None of these things can be done by the light tank alone. We must, therefore, have a considerable proportion of medium tanks – smaller [less tall], faster ones, armed with guns capable of knocking out any other tank and proof against the armour-piercing weapons of the light tank (Carey 1935: 745-746).

Production of Medium Mark IIs ended in 1934, upon the 200th vehicle. Given earlier write-offs, only 166 mediums were in service by 1935. In 1936, the government sent the Tank Brigade's only Light Battalion to Egypt (1st Battalion, RTC), reduced the Tank Brigade to three medium battalions (2nd, 3rd, 5th), and sent only medium tanks to complete the nascent battalion in Egypt (6th). On 20 November, at the annual Tank Corps Dinner, Liddell Hart heard officers doubting the wisdom of sending any light tanks abroad, which Liddell Hart took personally (note, 21 November 1936, LHCMA LH 11/1936/108).

In the same year, the government appropriated the funds for enough new medium-weight assault tanks (classified as "infantry tanks") to fill four "Army Tank Battalions" (4th, 7th, 8th, 9th RTC), and for the development of medium-weight screening and pursuit tanks (classified as "cruiser tanks"). Few would be received before the Second World War, so Vickers Mediums remained in service in Britain, Egypt, and India.

The Second World War proved that Liddell Hart was right, by the mid-1930s, to describe Vickers mediums as death traps, but disproved his confidence in lighter tanks and in tanks armed with just a medium machine-gun. His memoirs claim that he stood alone, from 1927 through 1929, for mixing "light and medium tanks," down to the company echelon, for deeper penetrative attacks, akin to the Blitzkrieg of 1939 to 1940. In fact, his publications of 1927 to 1929 advocate for mixing carriers and light tanks – the carriers as "stationary machine-gun nests" to suppress enemy anti-tank guns, the light tanks to assault those guns (1929c: 105; 1932c: 204, 209; 1935: 178, 183; 1965: I, 161, 178).

So far as Liddell Hart saw a need for medium tanks, he had wanted them to assault or simply occupy the objective, after tankettes and perhaps light tanks had "hosed" it with machine-gun fire. The British Army entered the Second World War with a peculiar assault class that it termed "infantry tank," actualized with both light and medium tanks, all prioritizing armor over lethality and mobility. Liddell Hart himself had contributed to this unbalance. The light infantry tank (Matilda I) accommodated only two men and a machine-gun, as he had always preferred for all tanks. The medium-weight alternative (Matilda II) accommodated four men, a two-pounder gun, and a machine-gun, and boasted thicker armor. Hobart's and Liddell Hart's opposition to these specifications contributed to under-investment and under-development, as explained in the next chapter.

This Matilda I is still in trials in July 1939.

CHAPTER 8

Infantry Tanks

In March 1934, the Financial Secretary to the WD, Duff Cooper MP, introduced the Army Estimates with a paraphrase of Liddell Hart's personal advice against thicker armor. "Armour-piercing bullets" are developing ahead of "bullet-resisting armour," Cooper said. In future years, "the most heavily armoured tanks" would be as vulnerable as "an old wooden caravan would be to the firing of today." In the press, Liddell Hart criticized Cooper's support for horse cavalry, but praised his preference for light tanks, although decades later he would claim to have criticized Cooper's scepticism of heavier tanks (1960: 185: 1965: I, 241).

In April 1934, Percy Hobart, as Inspector of the Royal Tank Corps, submitted to the Director of Military Training (DMT) a review of theories on infantry-support tanks. Without naming the protagonists, he described two schools of thought:

1. The "small tank school" (Martel and Liddell Hart) argues that many small, inconspicuous tanks with machine-guns should screen and support the infantry, particularly while infantrymen move their crew-served weapons to the flanks or rear of the enemy.

2. The "heavy tank school" argues that only well-gunned tanks (Hobart) or well-armored tanks (Hugh Elles, then Master General of the Ordnance, previously the first commander of the Tank Corps) could suppress entrenched defenders.

Missing from Hobart's paper is Fuller's requirement (since 1918) for a larger medium tank that could run faster, range further, and cross larger obstacles than prior tanks. Fuller classed his requirement as medium, and thought of the current Vickers Medium as light. For clarity, we should think of Fuller's requirement as heavy-medium, given the Army's eventual preference for "cruisers." The cruisers are light-mediums – fast enough for Fuller and Liddell Hart, but not robust enough for Fuller or Elles, and certainly not intended for assaults.

Hobart leaked to Liddell Hart his paper, but Liddell Hart paid little attention. He was confident he was winning the argument for light tanks in the press, and that Hobart would get over his anxiety for heavier armaments.

He paid even less attention to Macready, who took over SD2 in May. Macready preferred the "heavy tank school." He was appalled that the RTC's only new tanks were light, and that the cavalry still used horses (apart from two battalions of armored cars). He agreed that the cavalry requires fast light tanks for scouting and screening. Thus, his interim solution was to transfer light tanks from the RTC to the cavalry. But he wanted the RTC to receive heavy tanks to support infantry in the assault. However, he was directed to accommodate the cavalry's preference for pursuit and exploitation tanks. The infantry-support requirement was thrashed out by Hobart (representing the RTC), Martel (then studying at the Imperial Defence College, in expectation of promotion to the Directorate of Mechanization), and Liddell Hart (who was advising Cooper) (Macready 1965: 91). Over the summer, the requirement was split between fast light-mediums ("cruisers"), for pursuit and exploitation, and heavier mediums ("infantry tanks"), for support of infantry in the assault. Macready revealed the requirements to Liddell Hart on 13 November, and to RUSI on the next day.

> It has been decided that Army Tank Battalions are to be provided on the scale of one battalion per infantry division. The tank in these units would be of a different pattern to those in the Tank Brigade. Its role would be: to clear a passage through wire; to deal with unneutralized machine-guns; and to keep up the momentum of the infantry attack.
>
> The primary requirements of such armoured fighting vehicles are armour and inconspicuousness. Speed and radius of action will have to be sacrificed to some extent in order to obtain the necessary thickness of armour; while the armament will probably consist of machine-guns and anti-tank weapons. The tank itself is still in an experimental stage, but we hope that before very long it will be possible to go to production (Macready 1935: 11-12).

Liddell Hart was finishing a book at the time of Macready's briefing, in which he wrote of news that the army would be acquiring "special infantry tanks, low in speed as well as in build, but heavily armoured." He was referring to project A11, which would be produced (from late 1938), by Vickers, as the Matilda I. This is effectively a thickly-armoured light tank, since it accommodates just two men and a machine-gun. He interpreted it as fulfilling one of the roles for the tankette, i.e., close support of pedestrian infantry, although it is much slower than he wanted. His opposition to its pedestrian pace was certainly correct, although not for the right reason. The A11 could not fulfill his preferred role for tanks, i.e., fast raids on industrial and logistical targets. Thence, he warned that A11 could "not supersede the need for a proportion" of infantry to be mounted in machine-gun carriers. He preferred Martel's one-man "mechanical coffin." He wanted a battalion of carriers and light tanks for every two infantry battalions (1935: 264, 265, 271).

Since 1933, the RTC had been authorized with six battalions, but these remained equipped to less than half of authorized establishment. The 6th RTC had formed (in 1933) in Egypt, with just one company of mediums. The Tank Brigade (which assembled in April 1934) grew to four "mixed" (light/medium) battalions (2nd, 3rd, 4th, 5th) and a Light Battalion (1st). In late 1935, the Brigade lost 1st RTC to Egypt. In the new fiscal year (April 1936), the Brigade lost a mixed battalion (4th) to the new role of Army Tank Battalion. The 4th gave up its only medium company (to 6th RTC) in expectation of infantry tanks, so was left with only light tanks. By August, Hobart heard rumors that the 6th RTC would be brought back from Egypt for conversion to an Army Tank Battalion, and that two new Army Tank Battalions would be raised. Indeed, in September, a new government authorized four Army Tank Battalions (4th, 7th, 8th, 9th). However, only 4th held a cadre. In November, the Cabinet expected the second cadre to be created "shortly," but could not be sure, due to shortage of tank personnel. It would wait until May ("1st Tank Brigade 1936: 1st Sept. Signal Exercise," LHCMA Hobart; CIGS, "The Organization, Armament and Equipment of the Army," 16 November 1936, LHCMA Burnett-Stuart).

In October 1938, Vickers delivered the first full production Matilda I, when Liddell Hart realized how slow it really is.

> Deliveries of the first of the two types of infantry tank, the smaller of the two, are also increasing. These are heavily armoured machines, designed to give direct cover to the infantry attack by working with it; their role is thus more akin to that of the last war tank, and in their construction speed is subordinated to the thickness of armour (1939b: 322).

The pilot Matilda II (A12E1) was delivered in April 1938 for trials. In May, full production orders were placed. (Deliveries would arrive late, in September 1939.) Liddell Hart misreported that Matilda IIs were ordered at expense of artillery. Logically, he should have urged conversion of Army Tank Battalions to artillery, but he urged conversion to light tanks. In the 1950s, he admitted that "I never favoured the infantry tank, but merely regarded it as at best the lesser of two evils" (the greater evil being a heavy tank). His memoirs reveal his real concern: infantry tanks were acquired at expense of light tanks: "the only new tank battalions contemplated were to be for close support of the infantry instead of being a step towards forming any further tank brigades for mobile action." Yet his subsequent histories admit that Matilda IIs reigned supreme from 1939 to 1941 (1939b: 253, 296-297; to Ogorkiewicz, 2 July 1957, RACTM E2015.2015.64; 1965: I, 262; 1968: 760; 1970: 177).

In this admission, he effectively admits that he had pushed speed too far at the expense of armor. His obsession with speed was one driver towards the Army's late peacetime over-investment in cruiser tanks, as explained in the next chapter.

The 7th RTR shows off Matilda IIa tanks near Tobruk, in Libya, in September 1941. Matilda II tanks were last used in action in North Africa by the British on 22 July 1942. They remained in use with allies in Africa, the Middle East, Russia, Asia, and the Pacific Rim through the end of the war.

CHAPTER 9

Cruiser Tanks

Back when Liddell Hart first embraced an all-tracked offensive force, he aimed for a New Model Division with six battalions (more than half of the division's units) of "fast cruiser tanks of about 20 tons, well-armoured and with an armour-piercing gun as primary armament" (1924c: 45). Thus, he should have welcomed the light-medium tanks offered by Walter Christie of America – the smallest and fastest in their class, each weighing under 12 tons (without turret; Christie usually designed a turret ring in expectation that buyers would develop their own turrets). An American correspondent had sent reports since 1928. At the time, the M1928 accommodated two men, a mock machine-gun on top, and a mock 37-mm gun in the nose – choices that kept it under 6 feet in height and 10 long tons (11 short tons) in weight. It proved speeds of over 40 mph on tracks and 70 mph without tracks, far beyond Liddell Hart's specification. Yet he preferred smaller and lighter.

> As a substitute for existing armoured cars, it has certainly good scope, but as an "in-fighting" tank the comparatively large target it offers is a drawback, and it would seem to be rather a basis for further experiment than itself to be the tank type of the future (1932c: 129; 1935: 115).

Decades later, Liddell Hart would claim to have urged the War Department to consider the M1928 and, later, the M1930. He attributed the lack of evidence to his humility (to Ogorkiewicz, 30 August 1956, RACTM E2015.205.63; 1965: I, 390).

In fact, British acquisition of cruisers started in April 1936, when the latest "rearmament programme" became fiscally effective. The program included budgets for cruiser and infantry tanks. In October, Martel (then the Assistant Director of Mechanization) returned from Soviet demonstrations of "fast tanks" (abbreviated as "BTs" in Russian). The first BT was an imported Christie M1930 – an evolution from the M1928. Martel quickly escalated a request to import a M1930, in hope that that British derivatives would serve as "cruisers" – his new favorite requirement.

Martel leaked his report and requirement to Liddell Hart, who admitted his prior ignorance of the M1930. Like Martel, Liddell Hart favored anything faster and cheaper than the other medium tanks on offer (including infantry tanks), although Liddell Hart prioritized light tanks as smaller and cheaper still. From 30 to 31 October, *The Times* published his report, in two parts. The first part helpfully states that Britain's tank fleet is "insignificant compared with the importance of the role" and the "increasing threat" from "anti-tank weapons." The second part unhelpfully concludes "that hope lies only in swarms – to swamp the defence" ("Fifth Report of the Mechanization Board Covering the Period 1st January 1938 to 31st December 1938," RACTM E2010.1056; Martel to LH, 21 October 1936, LHCMA LH 1/492 Part 2; Liddell Hart 1939b: 321; 1965: I, 379-380).

In early 1937, he praised French "cavalry tanks," even though they are slower, thicker armoured, and better armed than British light tanks. Perhaps he ignored their specifications, in order to find fault with the British. He blamed the absence of similar tanks in Britain on "the characteristic British tendency to seek technical perfection instead of going into production as soon as it has found something that will be fairly effective."

Renault R35 tanks and horses in the Alps, circa 1937

However, his interest in mediums ebbed again. From mid-1937, he advised Belisha to acquire trucks, carriers, and light tanks for "armoured mobile" formations, and carriers for infantry formations. In September, he, Belisha, and other Francophiles travelled from the British to the French maneuvers. The French maneuvers included a battalion of new R35 tanks, In armament (short 37-mm gun), armor (43 mm), and speed (12 mph), the R35 sounds like an infantry tank, but in size, weight (11 metric tons), and crew (two) it resembles a light or light-medium. Still, Liddell Hart required them for British cavalry brigades, if not the Tank Brigade too (1937: 66, 72; 1965: II, 30; Minney 1961: 56-57; Colville 1972: 76-77).

In the next couple months, the General Staff were cowed by Belisha's purges and Liddell Hart's bad press. His nemesis at the time was John Burnett-Stuart, who was preparing for his final season at Southern Command, and in the Army, and was speaking freely. For 1937, he was directed to try 2nd Cavalry Brigade as an "armoured cavalry brigade." The brigade was trying four types of unit, equipped with, respectively: horses; trucks (carrying cavalrymen equipped as light infantry); armored cars, scout cars, and tracked carriers; and light tanks. He already wanted the cavalry to consolidate around one type of unit, in a reconnaissance role. He found its light tanks insufficiently stealthy and survivable. In conference with all officers, Burnett-Stuart observed that light tanks are small enough to hide behind the gentle rises of Salisbury Plain, but too conspicuous and vulnerable when reconnoitering, which usually ends in the loss of a tank. He suggested replacement of light tanks with cruiser tanks and motorcycle-sidecars (the latter armed with anti-tank rifles), and replacement of trucks with armored personnel carriers (armed with machine-guns). For now, he wanted to retain horsed cavalry in the infantry division's cavalry unit, for interoperability with most infantrymen (who walked) ("Southern Command Winter Exercise (The Mobile Division), 1936/1937: GOC-in-C's opening remarks at Scarborough," no date, and "Annual Report on Training of the Regular Army, 1936/1937," November 1937, LHCMA Burnett-Stuart).

Subsequently, on 18 November, Liddell Hart submitted an addendum to his earlier papers for Belisha. The addendum requires a "mobile" formation in Egypt, "mainly of cruiser tanks." Strangely, he continues to specify a mobile division at home with light tanks, presumably because he still imagines that anything heavier could not be enshipped or driven fast enough to avoid air attacks. Eventually, in January 1938, the General Staff (led since November by officers of his own recom-

Christie's turretless M1930 was designated A13E1 when tried by the British in November 1936.

Morris Motors delivered A13E2 for trials in October 1937. DDM derived this turret from the turret it had designed for A7E3.

The Morris-DDM A13E3 was first tried in February 1938. With minor changes, A13E3 was standardized as Cruiser III.

Two Cruiser IIs lead a Valentine I (an infantry tank derived from the Cruiser II) and two Matilda IIs at a RAOC Depot in August 1940.

mendation) stimulated a paper closer to their starting position than his own. Now, he specifies a mobile division with light tanks, light cruiser tanks, heavy cruiser tanks, and close-support (smoke) tanks. This was the first time Liddell Hart recognized the latter three classes (1939b: 288, 300).

The cruisers were still developmental, with low reliability and sustainability – partly inherent to the Christie tank from which almost all moving parts were developed, partly due to poorly-motivated suppliers, partly due to proliferation of suppliers. Martel was in charge of cruiser requirements, but his specifications and expectations remained vague, perhaps to avoid accountability. Still, he remained over-optimistic with everybody, which influenced Liddell Hart's reporting.

> So, working from the American Christie, we set out to develop one that would not only have a similar performance but a greater reliability. "Teething troubles," however, were numerous and prolonged before the new infant could be passed as satisfactory. Production is now proceeding. And the promise of the machines that are being delivered is backed by a comforting experience with the final pilot models, which had shown that they can maintain remarkably long daily mileages without giving trouble (1939b: 322).

Four cruiser types were developed at the same time. Nuffield Mechanization (a spin off from Morris Motors) developed light and heavy derivatives of the Christie M1930, within the same project (A13), which were eventually accepted into service as Cruiser III and Cruiser IV respectively. Vickers developed the (light) Cruiser I and (heavy) Cruiser II, within two prior projects (A9 and A10). The light cruisers were specified with the same armor as light tanks (14 mm). The heavy cruisers were differentiated by armor up to 30 mm thick. Otherwise, all mounted the same turret, designed by DDM. Liddell Hart's memoirs do not give the designations, names, classes, or specifications of these four products, but he refers to a successful "light medium" class, and takes credit for instigating it (1965: I, 391).

In fact, Nuffield's Cruisers were least reliable, because of Nuffield's under-investment, exclusion of War Department design authorities (except for the turret and fighting arrangements, which proved satisfactory), Martel's weak oversight, and Liddell Hart's urgency for faster tanks.

Derivatives were already in development, including a Cruiser V or Covenanter (A13 Mark III) (above). This was designed and developed by the Mechanization Board and London, Midland, & Scottish Railway (LMSR), with an unconventional automotive line. It would become the most over-produced of many undeployed British tank designs. It was piloted in November 1940, and soon condemned as useless below the turret for anything except training, but stayed in production until 1943. Nuffield's simultaneous Cruiser VI or Crusader, derived from Cruiser IV, looks little different but is slightly more reliable, thanks to minor automotive changes and an extra road wheel each side. Liddell Hart praised their speed, and ignored their poor reliability, survivability, and off-road mobility. Since he never attended any trials, his sole source of information was Martel. His earliest note on any technology in a cruiser dates to 1940, and focuses on the suspension, which enables exceptional speed for the class. In 1941, he archived an official document on defects in the trailing arm, but never publicly admitted any flaws in any cruisers.

All cruisers to date were armed with a tank version of the 40-mm two-pounder anti-tank gun. It fired faster projectiles than the 47-mm three-pounder, thanks to longer barrel and cartridges. However, its projectiles are smaller and lighter, and thus less destructive, even if more penetrative. Liddell Hart and Hobart had pressed for smaller caliber, so that more ammunition could be stowed internally (200 rounds by Hobart's unfulfilled specification), in hope of enabling the Tank Brigade to raid for days in the enemy rear without supply vehicles. The War Office judged the caliber too small to be worth procuring high-explosive rounds. Thus, cruisers were almost useless against the soft targets for which Hobart and Liddell Hart had required them. Cruisers were optimized to fight tanks, which Hobart and Liddell Hart wanted to evade without a fight. Matilda II mounted the same gun, and armor sufficient to defeat the same, but Hobart and Liddell Hart considered any fight between tanks as a distraction from raids on unarmored targets.

To improve lethality against soft targets, Hobart insisted that Cruiser I should carry two machine-gun turrets on the front hull, like Medium Mark III, but these were deleted to save weight and cost. He respecified the A8 (a long-running project by Vickers, incorporating DDM's three-man A7E3 turret) with a turret accommodating four, five, and eventually six men. A mock-up proved its impracticalities. Next, Hobart specified two machine-gun turrets ahead of the main turret on A8, A14 (by LMSR), and A16 (by LMSR and Nuffield). Their failures provoked him to specify two turrets atop the main turret of the A19. Neither Liddell Hart nor Hobart publicly admitted these failures, or their responsibility for pushing speed at the expense of lethality and survivability (LH 11/1940/110; LH 15/10/2; 1965: I, 392).

The 4th Battalion, Royal Northumberland Fusiliers, converted from machine-guns to motorcycles in 1938. Upon World War II, it mobilized as the reconnaissance unit for 50th Division, with 99 Norton motorcycle-sidecars, 43 solo motorcycles, and 88 cars and light trucks. Even counting medical, signals, supply, maintenance, kitchen, and command elements, it required about half as many personnel as an infantry battalion, which likely is another reason the type attracted Liddell Hart's endorsement. Here, two of the nine platoons (each 11 sidecars and one 15-hundredweight truck) pose for an official photographer in France in March 1940. Three sidecars in each platoon carry a Bren. Anti-tank rifles (23) were carried in trucks for distribution to defensive positions only. The unit's only armored vehicles were two-man Daimler Scout Cars, nominally 22 of them, but these remained short for years into the war.

CHAPTER 10

Motorcycles

Since the 1920s, German divisional reconnaissance units had used motorcycles, cars, and armored cars. Tanks were not available, given prohibitions agreed within the Treaty of Versailles in 1919.

In November 1937, Burnett-Stuart recommended motorcycle-sidecars (each armed with an anti-tank rifle) for the cavalry brigade, given their stealthiness next to light tanks, and to add some anti-tank capability to a brigade that otherwise mounted nothing heavier than machine-guns. At the end of the month, Belisha, with Liddell Hart's advice, purged the General Staff. Belisha tasked the new men with specifying Liddell Hart's papers on force structure, amongst other things. He did not want any replacement of light tanks, but suddenly liked motorcycles. In 1938, the War Office granted to each of the leading three reserve infantry divisions a battalion of motorcycles and motorcycle-sidecars, in lieu of light tanks. In 1939, Liddell Hart went further. He wanted every division (active and reserve) to receive a unit, and each field army HQ to hold several. This way, he released light tanks for the two "mobile divisions" (later: "armoured divisions") assembling that year. He rationalized that his requirement for tankettes had been fulfilled by the Bren Gun Carriers, and that motorcycles could range as freely as tankettes.

> A screen composed of motor-cyclist troops advancing by as many roads as possible, would form a modern application, to the approach march, of the swarm of skirmishers which preceded the Napoleonic columns in the attack. And by its capacity, through wide distribution, to explore the largest number of lines of advance simultaneously, it would also be of promise towards solving the problem of gaining ground quickly, and avoiding delays in the general advance, in face of the enemy's covering forces (1939b: 380).

Motorcycle-sidecars carry the same crewmen (two) as his preferred tanks, but only a Bren or a rifle as armament. Their clearer inferiorities are in survivability and mobility, although he did not admit any. Liddell Hart had justified light tanks and tankettes as fast, small, and mobile enough to evade enemies, so his endorsement of vehicles without armor or off-road mobility seems like a U-turn. The quote above suggests that he believed motorcycles would be so numerous and fast that they would not need armor.

He was wrong. In France, in 1940, British motorcycle-sidecars were too road-bound to avoid the enemy, too poorly armed to win a firefight, and too vulnerable to survive a firefight. Although German motorcycle-sidecars ranged free-er, given the disorganization and unreadiness on the Western Allied side, both armies soon restricted motorcycles to messaging, and converted divisional reconnaissance units to armored cars or light tanks. Liddell Hart ignored motorcycles after 1939. His histories do not mention British use, or his endorsement.

JS2s captured by the Germans in 1944.

A Centurion pilot, armed with 17-pounder gun and Polsten 20-mm cannon, in 1945.

CHAPTER 11

Future Tanks

After the Second World War, Liddell Hart rarely spoke about tank types or technologies, preferring to focus on his reinvention as the father of Blitzkrieg. He interpreted Blitzkrieg as fast and shocking, which justifies his prioritization of tank speed. However, he still over-played speed at the expense of lethality, survivability, and off-road mobility. He resented the trend to thicker armour and bigger guns, because weight trades against speed. Belatedly, he realized improvements in agility, thanks to developments in transmissions and differentials. He wrote that "manoeuvrability is even more important – for quickness in changing fire-positions and shortening the range, for more effective fire." He cites "the German Army['s]... most experienced tank leaders" (prisoners of war whom he had interviewed since 1945). Alas, he contradicts himself on the same page, and other pages, where he praises Soviet tanks for bigger guns than German competitors, but criticizes the current British Centurion tank as "reminiscent of the pedestrian and over-laden Roman legionary." In fact, the Centurion carried a smaller gun and thinner armour, but the same weight, as the Soviet JS2 tank – his favorite of the Second World War (1950: 175-176, 182, 235-236). The only explanation for this particular contradiction is his ongoing prejudice against the British General Staff. Worse, he claimed to know better than the users.

> The tendency was accentuated both by the infantry's constant cry for tank support and by the tank crews' cry for bigger and bigger tank guns. The less confidence these had in their own skill of maneuver, the more they clamoured for a decisively powerful gun, as well as thicker armour. So the tank itself grew bigger and heavier, while dwindling in manoeuvrable number...The compound effect of these factors was that, in the latter stages of the war, tank-battles declined into gun-duels between individual tanks or small units...It was "warfare with tanks," rather than "tank warfare" (1959: II, 455; 1960: 193-194).

How else are tanks supposed to duel, if not with their guns? This incongruity probably paraphrases a book that Liddell Hart had commissioned and edited before the war: "Duels, not only of isolated tanks against each other, but of small groups of tanks, will be a feature of such a war" (Sheppard 1938: 148-149).[*]

Meanwhile, Liddell Hart revived his wish for "swarms" of light tanks.

> Since armoured forces were first introduced into war their more convinced exponents have always insisted that their value essentially depended on their being employed "in swarms – to swamp the defence." It

---

[*] This echoes Fuller's (1920a: 315) prediction that "tank will meet tank." Liddell Hart analogized war to a duel: "War is a but a duel between two nations instead of two individuals" (1925: 75).

is the principle of saturation of confronting the defence with many more separate assailants than he can cope with...It would be wise to recognize that the present trend of mechanical design towards bigger tanks, and thus fewer of them, is unfavourable to the fulfilment of the principle. We might gain much by a fresh effort to develop a lighter and cheaper type of tank, provided that the importance of obstacle-crossing capacity is kept in mind. That requires length of chassis [actually, only for trench crossing], but not necessarily bulk or weight in proportion. Such tanks might mount rockets rather than a large-calibre gun – the Germans were going to concentrate on the production of rocket-tanks weighing under 20 tons if the war had continued [not true] (1950: 234-235).

He explicitly revived his pre-war advocacy for an independent brigade of light tanks. During the advance, these tanks would rely on "dispersion" and "fluidity" to avoid enemies. At the enemy's highest bases and HQs, they would suddenly concentrate. The fantasy assumes the enemy's incompetence at screening, defending, intercepting, and counter-attacking. Post-war, Liddell Hart assumes friendly aerial preponderance too. Before the war, he had assumed that light tanks could avoid enemy aircraft by speed and stealthiness. Presumably, he was corrected during the war by first German and later Western Allied aerial preponderance (1959: 456; 1960: 183, 195).

He adds new reasons to prefer light tanks. He mistakenly assumes that only light tanks could "move into cover before the [guided] missile arrives," and that only light tanks could open fire quicker than missile launchers. He does not specify their armament, but sometimes he seems to have only machine-guns in mind.

> The basic factors, and most distinctive features, in tank operations are speed and flexibility. These twin qualities are of more fundamental importance than the armour of the tank. They give its armament, which is not in itself unique, a unique quality in action...
>
> These twin qualities remain essential, and have even gained in importance, with the coming of nuclear weapons. For the military[**] problems of the present time, in a world that lies under the shadow of the catastrophic nuclear cloud, depend more than ever on the time-factor (1959: II, 451; 1960: 187-188).

Thus, he returns to speed as the priority. He requires "a lighter and nimbler type of tank" (1959: 458), "a lighter and cheaper type of tank" (1960: 198), and "high-speed tanks" (1968: 736). In the mix, he acknowledges "much to be said for...a hard core of heavy tanks." His proportions are the wrong way around. By then, main battle tanks (heavy tanks, by the standards of the Second World War) were predominant, and light tanks had been properly returned to their scouting and screening roles (except for a rarer role in support of air-deployed forces, which Liddell Hart never acknowledged).

His partial failure to learn the right lessons, and the partiality with which his wrong lessons were entertained, are best explained by his post-war role as official historian of the tank arm, as explained in the next chapter.

[**] In the second publication, "military" becomes "strategic" (1960a: 188).

CHAPTER 12

Official Historian of the Tank Arm

Liddell Hart's advocacy for tankettes, machine-gun carriers, light tanks, (light) cruiser tanks, and eventually motorcycles benefited the Cavalry arm most. The Cavalry was late to give up horses. Lighter vehicles matched its preferences for independent scouting, pursuit, and exploitation roles. And it ended up the larger user of tanks. From Spring 1939, the Royal Tank Corps was demoted to a Royal Tank Regiment (RTR), under a Royal Armoured Corps, in which cavalry units predominated (and still predominate).

By 1941, Liddell Hart's reputation and career in military affairs seemed finished. That year, he published only reprints and selective compendia of earlier writings. In 1944, the new Royal Armoured Corps Club appointed Fuller as one of its many Vice-Presidents, but ignored Liddell Hart (Tanks Victory Club 1946: 13, 34). Martel (1945: 17, 40) made clear that "it was mainly Major-General JFC Fuller who developed and built up these ideas" (armored warfare), and that although Liddell Hart had helped in the 1920s, he abandoned them in the 1930s. A separate wartime historian recalled Fuller as "the [only] pungent military writer" to "stigmatise" Britain's failure to acquire a mechanized army (Fairfax 1945: 48).

Percy Hobart did not care for public comment. In 1939, he had been dismissed from command of the nascent armoured division in Egypt (7th). He was recalled to command nascent divisions at home. His last command (79th) was administrative, not tactical, a home for engineering tanks – none categorized as light, none roled for raiding. It was abolished in August 1945. He prepared to retire in Spring 1946. Coincidentally, Liddell Hart finished a new book in August 1945, for publication in Spring 1946. It has nothing to do with tanks or maneuver warfare, but is incongruously dedicated "to PCS ('Patrick') Hobart in tribute to his dynamic contribution to the development of armoured mobility, and to his personal qualities as seen in 20 years' association" (1946: 6). The book does not mention Fuller or Martel.

In November 1945, the Director of the Royal Armoured Corps (DRAC) and staff agreed on an official history of the RAC, but none ever appeared. In early 1946, Charles Broad, then Representative Colonel-Commandant of the RTR, initiated a history of the RTC and RTR from 1916 to 1945, without the RAC. Broad negotiated with Liddell Hart, before appointing a "RTR History Committee" to manage the project. Its acknowledgements for the published work do not justify why Liddell Hart was chosen, except to mention that he had "for long been a friend of the Royal Tank Regiment" (1959: xi). His appointment was announced in the RAC Journal (October 1946), with the following anonymous justification:

> As a military historian, Captain Liddell Hart has a reputation second to none and he should prove an admirable choice as the writer of this history. For some years he was the military correspondent of The Times and he has written a number of books on military affairs which have made him well known not only in the Army, but to the general public as well.

This is all to the good, for the more the public knows about the Army the better, and a book by Liddell Hart should command a ready sale.

As in the 1920s, he was helped by the arm's desperation for good press, as it once again feared abolition. Yet he would ignore the commission for years, while he focused on a book about what German prisoners of war told him (1948). He leveraged much of the same content in his next book, and added his reinvention as an unbroken champion of the tank, and opponent of horse-cavalrymen, since 1919 (1950: 214-215).

In 1949, Hobart took over from Broad. Hobart had just renewed correspondence with Liddell Hart, after a crisis of confidence in his own legacy. Martel was unpersuaded. "For over 30 years there has been a small body in the Army, which was initiated by General (then Colonel) J.F.C. Fuller, whose views have been proved to be right to this day" (Martel to the editor of *The Times*, 11 August 1950: 46).

The RTR History Committee was an indulgent client. Nevertheless, Liddell Hart privately complained that "some of the members of the History Committee are very inclined to prefer pleasing legends to the truth." He blamed the Committee for lost maps and inaccurate regimental appendices. His greatest grievance was its delegation of proof-reading to "numerous commanders" (to Hotblack, 9 January 1958, RACTM Hotblack 2; to Hamish Hamilton, 7 October 1958, Bristol University Library Special Collections, DM1352/I.i.).

The history was published a decade late, in 1959, with only his name on the title page, even though dozens of men had written and edited it. Liddell Hart is best described as editor-in-chief. Tank officers were seconded to help. He consulted many others. He never consulted Fuller, but unadmittedly relied on Fuller's histories of the First World War. He ignored tank engineers, even though some survived from the First World War.

From 1950 to 1951, the RTR seconded two research assistants (Captain Norman Sims and Lieutenant-Colonel Colin Paddock), who soon started to write chapters for themselves. Hobart remained the project manager until the end, although with declining influence. As the project dragged on, Hobart prevailed on more officers to write or review chapters. Hobart prodded Liddell Hart to contact Brigadier Michael Carver, who had joined the Tank Corps in the 1930s, served under Hobart in 1945, and renewed correspondence with Hobart from 1950. By then, Carver had been appointed by the General Staff to investigate tank qualities, for which he compiled tables of data on tanks and guns. Within years, Carver was a published historian in his own right. While reviewing Liddell Hart's latest book, Carver inadvertently cast doubt on Liddell Hart's claims to influence the Germans. Liddell Hart's recriminations eventually convinced Carver that Liddell Hart was hiding something. Thence, Carver realized his patchy knowledge and agendas (Carver 1989: 292-293).

On the data, Liddell Hart abandoned Carver for Major-General Nigel Duncan, who succeeded Hobart as the RTR's Colonel-Commandant from January 1952, until retirement in August. (Duncan succeeded Hobart as Lieutenant-Governor of the Royal Hospital Chelsea in October 1953.) In August 1952, while Liddell Hart was away in America, Hobart asked retired Major E.W. "Shep" Sheppard – a long-time collaborator of Liddell Hart's – to author several chapters on the North African and Italian campaigns of the Second World War. Hobart hoped that Liddell Hart would return to the commission in November 1952, but Liddell Hart did not. Meanwhile,

Hobart passed Sheppard's chapters to Carver and Major-General Pete Pyman (another tank officer). Hobart was desperate: "I'm afraid I agree with you about the dry bones. I was most reluctant to bring in anyone else, but BLH had been six years at the job and I would like to see the book published before I die" (to Carver, 3 and 15 September 1952, RACTM 1968.30.16). Months later, Hobart asked a wider circle of peers to review and edit the "dull" and "long" chapters on the Italian campaign. "The fact is one has to be a born author to be able to do it the way Liddell Hart does" (to George W. Richards, 4 May 1953, RACTM E2004.1278). Yet Hobart soon realized that Liddell Hart was as wordy and sketchy as Sheppard.

> I am afraid that your criticism of his "asides" (e.g., two pages on the German campaign in Poland) which have no bearing on the RTR at all, will fall on deaf ears. He simply will not excise; and when one insists on cutting down, is absolutely and uncontrollably pious. Well, all artists must resent what they regard as the mutilation of their children. And one has to accept this as part of the price of genius, well, if not genius, exceptional talent.

> He now won't allow me to see what he writes; always finds some excuse. So the day when the whole MSS is dumped on me, with I've no doubt a take-it-or-leave-it challenge, will be a fête day. The fireworks will follow when "the vets" begin to advise curtailment as essential to publication in a single volume (Hobart to Carver, 4 August 1953, RACTM E1968.30.16).

By the last month of 1953, Hobart judged "that we are in sight of the end." He blamed delays on Liddell Hart's seasonal illnesses and "dissatisfaction" (Hobart to Carver, 30 November 1953, RACTM E1968.30.16). In fact, the book was still years away from publication.

Liddell Hart had spent seven years on the book by 1954, when the RTR History Committee started publishing extracts in the RTR's own journal. In September, Martel complained about Liddell Hart's draft account of the battle at Arras in May 1940, where Martel had commanded a division. They had not spoken about it since 1947. Liddell Hart blamed the collective, so Martel blamed Hobart.

> If the rest of the history is like these two extracts, the right thing would be stop publication while the mistakes are rectified, but I hope that these two extracts were just unfortunate ones. We surely do not want a heavy criticism of the RTR history. I now see why Hobo refused to let me see the drafts. His action was just childish. I feel sure that you will get all this right before publication but it will need strong action on the part of someone (Martel to LH, 16 September 1954, RACTM E2006. 738).

Liddell Hart was playing Martel and Hobart against each other. He consulted Martel on the tank technologies of the First World War, while complaining to others about Martel's contradictions (LH to Ogorkiewicz, 9 October 1956, RACTM E2015.2015.63). The consultation appeased Martel for a couple years. Subsequently, Martel realized Liddell Hart's duplicity.

> After the Second World War, General Broad asked me if I would read the proofs and I replied that I would willingly do so. I naturally had a very wide and detailed knowledge of the RTR. When General Hobart became

representative Commandant however I found that I could make no contact with the committee that was dealing with this, though I tried several times. As a result my very wide knowledge of the facts was completely excluded from consideration for the history, though I did send some files to Liddell Hart.

The main point on which some of us feel very concerned is about the references in the history to the action taken by very senior officers in connection with General Hobart [especially his dismissal from service] (Martel to Committee of the RTR history, circa 1958, RACTM Briggs).

Liddell Hart came to rely upon Richard Ogorkiewicz, a young civilian automotive engineer with a side interest in the history of tanks. Ogorkiewicz published on tanks first in 1948 (on Soviet tanks, in the RAC Journal). He first contacted Liddell Hart in July 1949, for access to Liddell Hart's sources on tanks. Liddell Hart replied to ask for sources useful to the official history. By the mid-1950s, he used the young man as his primary source for technical information. Most subjects were weapons developed in Britain during the inter-war period, about which Ogorkiewicz (who was born in 1926 in Poland) had originally contacted Liddell Hart.

Liddell Hart came to trust Ogorkiewicz over the tank officers, although he sometimes blamed Ogorkiewicz for not spotting discrepancies in their data (to Ogorkiewicz, 23 June 1953, RACTM E2015.2015.61; 3 September, 15 and 30 October, and 9 November 1956, RACTM E2015.2015.63; 13 November and 10 December 1957, RACTM E2015.2015.64). By 1958, Ogorkiewicz was the lead writer of the technical specifications and the only tabulator of the data on tanks and guns, with which Liddell Hart had been struggling for years. Ogorkiewicz's main source was a table drawn up by the School of Tank Technology in 1951. However, Liddell Hart denigrated its reliability, perhaps mistaking it for Carver's work (to Ogorkiewicz, 4 February and 28 March 1958, RACTM E2015.2015.65). Ogorkiewicz complained to Carver that Liddell Hart was appropriating and disrespecting their work:

> [T]he table of tanks is mostly mine, that of tank guns entirely[,] and – I have just looked – I have one copy-sheet of comments on the final version alone. Not, of course, that Liddell Hart accepted all my comments, any more than anyone else's I suppose. For instance, I was against his misleading aside about Polish cavalry charges on p. 4 vol. II but it is still there. However, so far as I can be impartial, I consider "The Tanks" a very valuable historical work but somewhat uneven in the quality of its contents and in the coverage of the different periods. To me the best parts are the descriptions of the Desert and Normandy campaigns; that of the World War I tank actions is also good but then one has seen most of it elsewhere, even if not as meticulously presented. The development of the first tanks is well covered and I am glad that Liddell Hart has given due credit to the RNAS [Royal Naval Air Service], thus correcting the common impression that it was all [Ernest] Swinton's idea. Tank development of the mid-thirties is also good but, in contrast, the 1939-45 tank development is very sketchily treated (Ogorkiewicz to Carver, 20 March 1959, RACTM E2015.2015.5).

Ogorkiewicz wrote this privately, at the time of publication. Publicly, he whitewashed the official history. After all, Liddell Hart's reputation reflected on his own.

> My early visits to the Tank Museum involved helping officers at what was then the School of Tank Technology, also located at the Royal Armoured Corps Centre and responsible at the time for running the museum, to collect information about tanks for the history of the Royal Tank Regiment (RTR) which Captain B.H. Liddell Hart (later Sir Basil Liddell Hart), the world famous military thinker and historian, was asked to write. This took several years but when the two volume history of the RTR was published in 1959 under the title "The Tanks" Liddell Hart very generously acknowledged in it my help (2021: 18).

Ogorkiewicz and Liddell Hart remained somewhat co-dependent. Liddell Hart invited Ogorkiewicz to write a chapter on Soviet tanks for a book on "The Soviet Army," edited by Liddell Hart (1956). Ogorkiewicz took advice and help from Liddell Hart on book publishers (to Liddell Hart, 7 September 1958, RACTM E2015.2015.65). Liddell Hart volunteered to find a job at Vickers or Chrysler (to Ogorkiewicz, 6 July 1954, RACTM E2015.2015.62). He wrote recommendations for official jobs too (to DGFV, 2 January 1957, RACTM E2015.2015.64; to the MCS, 9 January 1962, RACTM, E2015.2015.69). He intervened with official authorities when Ogorkiewicz did not get a job (to Ogorkiewicz, 25 May 1963, RACTM E2015.2015.72).

The galley proofs reached Liddell Hart from November to December 1957. His commission had lasted almost 13 years when the two volumes were published in January 1959. His preface admits that "I have spent a far longer time on this book than on any previous one, and am still far from content" (1959: xiii).

For all the years of preparation, Liddell Hart produced an egocentric, patchy history, often more like a memoir or polemic. His only references to tank types are passing judgments, such as "satisfactory" or "old." He worked most on the chapters covering the interwar years. These chapters muse on history as a clash of personalities, with frequent references to his own guiding hand. He ignores organizational structures and processes, except to mention when certain personalities were appointed to certain positions. He retails the lie that the British elite neglected himself, Broad, and Hobart, while Germans implemented their ideas. The rest of the first volume pretends that Lindsay, Broad, and Hobart were the most progressive soldiers, guided throughout by Liddell Hart personally. He briefly praises "Fuller's vision, and prophetic activity…from 1920 onwards" (when Fuller was in the War Office's SD4 – a doctrine and training department). He ignores Fuller's role from 1918 to 1920 at SD7 (a tank requirements department). He falsely claims credit for persuading George Milne (CIGS) to appoint Fuller as Military Assistant in 1926 (1959: I, 201, 234). Liddell Hart's most focused assessment of Fuller seems more like self-promotion (Danchev 1998: 120).

> As has frequently happened, a great opportunity found a man of genius to match it, with results that profoundly affected the subsequent course of history. The turn they ultimately took was not what he had hoped, but this was due to his countrymen's neglect of the old warning that "a prophet is not without honour save in his own country." The British Army has thrown up a number of unusual men who have been fertile in ideas,

> but none have been so fruitful as Fuller, or borne fruit so widely – he was the first who ever made the heads of Continental armies look to England for professional guidance. If the survey be extended to cover the whole military world, critical examination of all the soldiers who have left their mark on events shows none of such imaginative power or mental range – judged by their recorded thoughts. There were flaws in his logic and gaps in his vision, but that was true also of Clausewitz, and of Napoleon, while neither of these two outstanding peaks of the military profession – in thought, and its application – matched him in progressiveness and far-sightedness.
>
> It was the Army's loss and England's, that his executive opportunities were brief, and limited in scope, for his use of them had been striking as far as it went. But his conceptive powers could not be circumscribed, and they proved of more far-reaching effect than any modern soldier has achieved by action (1959: I, 220-221).

Fuller charitably reviewed the work as Liddell Hart's "masterpiece, not because of his enormous industry, his deep understanding of war, and the care with which he has sifted his evidence, but because in the interim war years he played so prominent a part in shaping tank theory, tactics[,] and training." Nevertheless, Fuller named Hobart, Broad, Lindsay, and Martel as the saviors of the tank arm between the world wars. In his next book, Fuller generously cites Liddell Hart's history as a source for Fuller's description of the tank battles of the First World War, even though Fuller's own books were the sources for Liddell Hart's history (The Spectator, 30 January 1959: 36; 1961: 175).

Lieutenant-General H.G. Martin admired the history but not the author. He acknowledged that the book was "acute and detailed. Some readers, however, may find slightly irritating his habit of quoting *obiter dicta* of German generals as though they were the Tables of the Law" ("Tanks Yesterday and Tomorrow," Daily Telegraph, 15 January 1959: 19). Bernard Fergusson described the book as "at once a labour of love and a bundle of whips and scorpions: a stimulating and satisfying mixture."

> One need not subscribe to all Captain Liddell Hart's judgments and prejudices; but the precision with which he has built up his charges of gross obstinacy on the part of high military authority between the wars is deadly and damning (Sunday Times, 25 January 1959: 33).

David Zook (1960: 189) contrasted Liddell Hart's egocentric narrative with Fuller's "thorough" research, "painstaking documentation", and "ability to interpret and analyze data."

J.P. Harris, being ignorant of Liddell Hart's co-authors, attributed his merits to official oversight and public scrutiny.

> It must be recognized, however, that Liddell Hart's monumental The Tanks, his history of the Royal Tank Regiment and its antecedents, is in most respects a very good book, possibly his best. This discipline of writing regimental history, which involved submitting his drafts for scrutiny by the regiment's representatives, seemed to have forced him to stick to

the facts more and ride his hobby-horses less than he did in many of his other writings. The Tanks, though undocumented [uncited], is a work of impressive scholarship and, while its interpretations are sometimes questionable, is generally accurate in matters of fact (Harris 1995: 1).

More technically-engaged historians observed that "Liddell Hart's work on the Royal Tank Regiment [was] clearly designed to demonstrate the infallibility of the author's opinion" (Hughes, Broshot, and Philson 1999: 122).

Soon, the RTR published *A Short History of the RTR*, by Kenneth Macksey who had joined the RTR in 1944. A comrade described it as "a much easier [to] read production than the official history." Later, Macksey completed unofficial histories of the RTR from 1945 to 1975, and of the RTC, RTR, and RAC from 1914 to 1975. Throughout, he makes no references to Liddell Hart's history, even though he admired Liddell Hart in person (Macksey 1965; George A. Storrar to Macksey, 4 June 1966, RACTM E2002.986; Macksey 1975; Macksey 1983).

Elliot Hotblack, who had served with Fuller and Martel on the Tank Corps staff, complained that Liddell Hart's and "previous histories over-stressed the incompetence of our own higher command and under-valued the preparedness and strength of the Germans." Hotblack welcomed a new history of the RTC and RTR by Sergeant Kenneth Chadwick of the RAC Depot Bovington – part of a series on 'Famous Regiments" under the guidance of General Brian Horrocks. Chadwick's book received little notice (Hotblack to Chadwick, 22 May 1968 and 20 July 1970, RACTM Hotblack 1; Chadwick 1970).

Liddell Hart died in 1970, with his reinvention as the constant champion of the Tank Corps, and critic of the cavalry, intact. Eighteen years later, John Mearsheimer (1988: 24-30) pointed out the falsity of this reinvention, but, like all contemporaries, ignored Liddell Hart's record on tanks themselves.

Liddell Hart's thinking about tanks is anchored in his traumatic experience of the Great War. Desperate to avoid another, he hoped that stealthiness and speed could lower exposure and quicken victories and thence lower casualties. His theory is correct. His application is not. At first, he reduced the arms to lighter infantry, except for an unarmed carrier for each platoon's equipment. In the 1920s, Fuller persuaded him to embrace mechanized combined arms (1925). However, his hopes for stealthiness and speed lingered. Unwilling to fully study the techniques and technologies, he mistook one-man tankettes as stealthy and fast enough to become the means of his theory. He reduced mobility to speed, treated speed as sufficient for survivability, and imagined that light and medium machine-guns are sufficient to defeat all other weapons. By the 1930s, he realized the superior mobility of light tanks, but still specified only two men and a machine-gun, in order to keep them small and fast, and thence (he assumed) practically as stealthy and survivable as tankettes. He rejected more crewmen and larger armaments, because larger tanks are heavier and thence slower and more exposed, all other things equal. He saw no need for tanks to fight anything but industrial and logistical targets, so prioritized evasion over confrontation. He saw no need for combined arms, and thus resented infantry tanks. He saw no need for medium tanks, until the promise of fast cruiser tanks. Ultimately, his pursuit of stealthiness and speed led him to motorcycles, with no armor and less lethality than a tankette. Liddell Hart proved the ideals of speed and stealthiness, but we should apply them more realistically.

REFERENCES

Bidwell, Reginald George Shelford (1973). Modern Warfare: A Study of Men, Weapons and Theories. London: Allen Lane.

Bond, Brian (1977). Liddell Hart: A Study of his Military Thought, London: Cassell.

Carey, B. (1935). Whither the Tank Brigade? Journal of the Royal United Service Institution, 80/520: 745-748.

Chadwick, Kenneth (1970). The Royal Tank Regiment, London: Leo Cooper.

Colville, John Rupert (1972). Man of Valour: The life of Field-Marshal the Viscount Gort, London: Collins.

Danchev, Alex (1998). Alchemist of War: The Life of Basil Liddell Hart, London: Weidenfeld & Nicolson.

Fuller, J.F.C. (1920). Tanks in the Great War, 1914-1918, London: John Murray.

- (1926). The Foundations of the Science of War, London: Hutchinson.

- (1932). Lectures on F.S.R. III (Operations Between Mechanized Forces), London: Sifton, Praed.

- (1936). Memoirs of an Unconventional Soldier, London: Ivor Nicholson & Watson.

- (1937). Towards Armageddon: The Defence Problem and its Solution, London: Lovat Dickson.

- (1943). Armored Warfare: An Annotated Edition of Lectures on FSR III, Harrisburg, Pennsylvania: Military Service Publishing Company.

Gat, Azar (1998). Fascist and Liberal Visions of War: Fuller, Liddell Hart, Douhet, and Other Modernists, Oxford, England: Clarendon Press.

- (2000). British Armour Theory and the Rise of the Panzer Arm: Revising the Revisionists, Houndmills: Macmillan Press.

Harris, J. Paul (1995). Men, Ideas and Tanks: British Military Thought and Armoured Forces, 1903-1939, Manchester University Press.

Howard, Michael, ed. (1965c). The Theory and Practice of War: Essays Presented to Captain B.H. Liddell Hart on his Seventieth Birthday, London: Cassell.

- (1979). "The Fuller-Liddell Hart Lecture," RUSI Journal, 124/1: 21-31.

Hughes, David, James Broshot, and Alan Philson (1999). The British Armies in World War Two: An Organizational History, Volume 1, British Armoured and Cavalry Divisions, West Chester, Ohio: George F. Nafziger.

Liddell Hart, Adrian (1953). Strange Company, London: George Weidenfeld & Nicolson.

Liddell Hart, Basil H. (1918a). Outline of the New Infantry Training, Adapted to the Use of the Volunteer Force, Cambridge University Press.

- (1918b). New Methods in Infantry Training, Cambridge University Press.

- (1918c). Battle Drill, or Attack Formations Simplified, Cambridge University Press.

- (1919a). "The 'Ten Commandments' of the Combat Unit: Suggestions on its Theory and Training," RUSI Journal, 64/454: 288-293.

- (1919b). "Suggestions on the Future Development of the Combat Unit: The Tank as a Weapon of Infantry," RUSI Journal, 64/456: 666-669.

- (1920a). "The Essential Principles of War and Their Application to the Offensive Infantry Tactics of Today," United Service Magazine, 61/1097: 30-44.

- (1920b). "The 'Man-in-the-Dark' Theory of War: The Essential Principles of Fighting Simplified and Crystallized into a Definite Formula," National Review, 75/448: 473-484.

- (1920c). "A New Theory of Infantry Tactics Based on a Direct Application of the 'Man-in-the-Dark' Theory of War," National Review, 75/449: 693-702.

- (1921a). "The 'Man-in-the-Dark' Theory of Infantry Tactics and the 'Expanding Torrent' System of Attack," RUSI Journal, 66/461: 1-23.

- (1921b). "A Science of Infantry Tactics," The Royal Engineers Journal, 33/4: 169-182.

- (1922a). "A Study of the New French Infantry Regulations," The Royal Engineers Journal, 35/5: 233-256.

- (1922b). "Are Infantry Doomed?" The National Review, 79/471: 455-463.

- (1922c). "Infantry – 'The New Model'," The National Review, 79/473: 712-722.

- (1922d). "The Future Development of Infantry," The National Review, 80/476: 286-294.

- (1922e). "Colonel Bond's Criticisms (A Reply)," The Royal Engineers Journal, 36/5: 297-309.

- (1922f). "A Study of the French 'FSR' – Instruction Provisoire Sur L'Emploi Tactique Des Grandes Unités," RUSI Journal, 67/468: 666-677.
- (1923a). "Study and Reflection v. Practical Experience: A Critical Examination of the Claims of Age, the Professional, and the 'Practical' Soldier to Unique Authority on War," Army Quarterly, 6/2: 318-331.
- (1923b). A Science of Infantry Tactics Simplified, London: William Clowes & Sons.
- (1924a). "The Next Great War," Royal Engineers Journal, 38/1: 90-107.
- (1924b). "Two Great Captains: Jenghiz Khan and Subutai," Blackwood's Magazine, 215/1303: 644-659.
- (1924c). "The Development of the 'New Model' Army," Army Quarterly, 9/1: 37-50.
- (1925). Paris or the Future of War, London: Kegan Paul.
- (1927a). "The Army of a Nightmare," The Fighting Forces, in 1941a: 69-81.
- (1927b). The Remaking of Modern Armies, London: John Murray.
- (1927c). Great Captains Unveiled, W. Blackwood and Sons, London.
- (1927d). "Back to Armour: Sir George Milne and Future Warfare – The Power of Petrol," Royal Tank Corps Journal: 191-192.
- (1927e). "Army Training, 1927," RUSI Journal, 72/488: 746-754
- (1929a). The Decisive Wars of History: A Study in Strategy, Boston: Little, Brown, & Company.
- (1929b). Sherman: Soldier, Realist, American, Boston: Dodd, Mead & Company.
- (1929c). "The New British Doctrine of Mechanized War," The English Review, in 1941a: 92-107.
- (1930a). Sherman: The Genius of the Civil War, London: Benn.
- (1930b). The Real War, 1914-1918, London: Faber & Faber.
- (1930c). "The Army Exercises of 1930," RUSI Journal, 75/500: 681-690.
- (1932a). "War and Peace," English Review, 54: 438-440.
- (1932b). "Aggression and the Problem of Weapons," English Review, 55: 71-78.
- (1932c). The British Way in Warfare, London: Faber & Faber.
- (1932d). "The Tale of the Tank," The Nineteenth Century and After, 112: 595.
- (1933a). "The Grave Deficiencies of the Army," The English Review, 56: 147-
- (1935). When Britain Goes to War: Adaptability and Mobility, London: Faber & Faber.
- (1936a). The War in Outline, 1914-1918, London: Faber & Faber.
- (1936b). "Future Warfare," The Atlantic Monthly, 158: 687-695.
- (1937). Europe in Arms, London: Faber & Faber.
- (1938a). Through the Fog of War, New York: Random House.
- (1938b). T.E. Lawrence to His Biographer Liddell Hart, London: Faber & Faber.
- (1939a). "Britain is in Danger," Evening Standard, in 1941: 126-133.
- (1939b). The Defence of Britain, London: Faber & Faber.
- (1940). "The Best Guarantee Against Aggression," in 1941: 164-168).
- (1941). The Current of War, London: Hutchinson.
- (1944). Thoughts on War, London: Faber & Faber.
- (1946). The Revolution in Warfare, London: Faber & Faber.
- (1948). The Other Side of the Hill: Germany's Generals, Their Rise and Fall, with their own Account of Military Events, London: Cassell,.
- (1950). Defence of the West, London: Cassell.
- (1951). The Other Side of the Hill, revised edition, London: Cassell.
- (1952). "The Objective in War: National Object and Military Aim," Naval War College Review, 5/4: 1-30.
- (1953). The Rommel Papers, London: Collins.
- ed. (1956). A Battle Report: Alam Halfa, Quantico, VA: Marine Corps Association.
- (1959). The Tanks: The History of the Royal Tank Regiment and its Predecessors Heavy Branch Machine-Gun Corps Tank Corps and Royal Tank Corps, 1914-1945, London: Cassell.
- (1960). Deterrent or Defence: A Fresh Look at the West's Military Position, London: Stevens & Sons.
- (1965). The Memoirs of Captain Liddell Hart, London: Cassell.
- (1968). "The Second World War," in Mowat 1968: 735-797.
- (1970). History of the Second World War, London: Cassell,.

Luvaas, Jay (1964). The Education of an Army: British Military Thought, 1815-1940, Chicago University Press.

Macksey, Kenneth (1965). To the Green Fields Beyond: A Short History of the Royal Tank Regiment, Bovington: Royal Tank Regiment.
- (1979). The Tanks: History of the Royal Tank Regiment, 1945-1975, Arms & Armour Press.
- (1983). A History of the Royal Armoured Corps and its Predecessors, 1914-1975, Beaminster, England: Newtown Publications.

Macready, Gordon N. (1935). "The Trend of Organization in the Army," The Journal of the Royal United Service Institution, 80/517: 1-20.

- (1965). In the Wake of the Great, London: William Clowes & Sons.

Martel, Giffard le Quesne (1927). Report on the Staff Conference held at the Staff College, Camberley, 17th to 20th January, 1927, London: His Majesty's Stationary Office.

- (1931). In the Wake of the Tank: The First Fifteen Years of Mechanization in the British Army, London: Sifton Praed.

- (1945). Our Armoured Forces, London: Faber & Faber.

- (1949). An Outspoken Soldier: His Views and Memoirs, London: Sifton Praed.

Mearsheimer, John J. (1988). Liddell Hart and the Weight of History, Ithaca, NY: Cornell University Press.

Minney, R.J. (1961). The Private Papers of Hore-Belisha. Garden City, NY: Doubleday.

Newsome, Bruce Oliver (2021a). The Rise and Fall of Western Tanks, I, 1855-1939, Coronado, California: Tank Archives Press.

- (2021b). The Rise and Fall of Western Tanks, II, 1939-1955, Coronado, California: Tank Archives Press.

- (2023). A Practical Introduction to Security and Risk Management, Coronado, CA: Perseublishing.

- (2024a). Basil Liddell Hart: Life, Thought, Legacy, Coronado, CA: Perseublishing.

- (2024b). Tank Raids and Blitzkrieg: The Development and Misrepresentation of Maneuver Warfare Since 1919, Coronado, CA: Perseublishing.

Noel-Baker, Philip John (1936). The Private Manufacture of Armaments, London: Victor Gollancz.

- (1979). The First World Disarmament Conference, 1932-1933: And Why it Failed, Oxford: Pergamon Press.

Ogorkiewicz, Richard M. (2021). Observer of Cold War Tank Development, Bovington: The Tank Museum.

Pile, Frederick (1949). Ack-Ack: Britain's Defence against Air Attack During the Second World War, London: George G. Harrap.

- (1965). "Liddell Hart and the British Army, 1919-1939" in Howard 1965: 169-183.

Reid, Brian Holden (1987). J.F.C. Fuller: Military Thinker, London: Macmillan Press.

Ross, Gordon MacLeod (1976). The Business of Tanks, 1933 to 1945, Ilfracombe, England: Arthur H. Stockwell.

Sheppard, E. W. (1938). Tanks in the Next War, The Next War Series, edited by Liddell Hart, London: Geoffrey Bles.

Tanks Victory Club (1946). Twenty-Five Thousand Tanks: A Record of the War Effort of Those Who Provided the "Armour in which We Trusted", London: Tanks Victory Club.

Temperley, Arthur C. (1938). The Whispering Gallery of Europe, London, Collins.

Trythall, Anthony John, "Boney" Fuller: Soldier, Strategist, and Writer, 1878-1966, New Brunswick, NJ: Rutgers University Press, 1977.

Wright, Patrick (2000). Tank: The Progress of a Monstrous War Machine, New York: Viking.

Zook, David H. (1960). "John Frederick Charles Fuller, Military Historian," Military Affairs, 23/4: 185-193.

www.ingramcontent.com/pod-product-compliance
Lightning Source LLC
Chambersburg PA
CBHW061804070526
44586CB00023B/2714